THE AFFLUENT INVESTOR

THE AFFLUENT INVESTOR
Investment Strategies
for All Markets

Stephen P. Rappaport

New York Institute of Finance

Library of Congress Cataloging-in-Publication Data

Rappaport, Stephen P.
    The affluent investor: investment strategies for all markets /
Stephen P. Rappaport.
        p.   cm.
    ISBN 0-13-018375-X
    1. Investments.   2. Securities.   3. Portfolio management.
    I. Title.
    HG4521.R286   1990
    332.6—dc20   89-28786
                                                                  CIP

Printed in the United States of America
10   9   8   7   6   5   4   3   2   1

New York Institute of Finance
(NYIF Corp.)
2 Broadway
New York, New York 10004-2207

To my mother, Claire Ruth Rappaport, not only for all the obvious reasons, but also for many others that are much more important—at least, to me.

Acknowledgments

Recognizing one's associates who have aided an author in a self-imposed literary task, regardless of the extent to which they did, is a moment of significance in two senses. In one way, it signals somewhat conclusively, and often times rather happily, that the curtain is being drawn on the production of a book's manuscript. As such, it is an exhilarating experience for the author who perhaps long ago began work on a text with at times little hope that it would be completed, that it would be a significant contribution to a given field, or that it would even be well received, noting that the latter two may not necessarily go hand in hand. In another sense, it is a rather nostalgic time. It allows, and in a few cases no doubt forces, the author to spend time reviewing the circumstances surrounding the writing of the volume. This process inevitably brings to mind all of those who have knowingly or unknowingly made contributions of all sorts to the book and deserve some special words of appreciation from the author in acknowledgment form.

Although the limitations of space do not afford writers the opportunity to recognize all those who share the thread of commonality sewing together all that goes into the production of a book, there are a few colleagues whose impact, through their encouragement and support on this and other related works, bears mention.

These individuals include: Edward I. O'Brien, President, Securities Industry Association; George Ball, James Tozer, James Gahan, James Barton, Leland Paton, Howard Whitman, Herbert Finn, Gerald McBride, and John Glidden of Prudential-Bache Securities Inc.; Richard West, Robert Lamb, and Robert Kuhn of the New York University Graduate School of Business Administration; William Sharwell, George Parks, Arthur Centonze, Clarke Johnson, Verne Atwater, George Matson, Basheer Ahmed, James Hall, and Kenneth Halcott of the Lubin Graduate School of Business, Pace University; Walter Stursberg, Olshan, Grundman & Frome, Esqs.; Michael Minter, Shearson Lehman Hutton Inc.; Diane Sine, Morgan Stanley & Co.; David Darst, Goldman, Sachs & Co.; Thomas Monti, Bankers Trust Company; and Richard Poirier, Lazard Frères & Co.

Others who have provided encouragement are: Samuel Hayes III, Harvard Business School; Burton Malkiel, Princeton University; John Harbison, Booz•Allen & Hamilton Inc.; Marc Schwarz, Touche Ross & Co.; Sharon Sager, Kidder, Peabody & Co.; Emma Hill, Wertheim & Co., Inc.; Clifton Fenton, John Nuveen & Co.; Barbara Collins, Bank of New York; Douglas Rogers, Baring Brothers & Co., Inc.; and Jeffrey Liddle, Liddle, O'Connor, Finkelstein & Robinson, Esqs.

Over the years, a tremendous amount of support and encouragement for my investment-related projects has come from professionals associated with "Camp Wonderful" in the Hamptons on Long Island, in New York. As a result, it is fitting that I acknowledge the following principals: Richard Mayberry, Citicorp Venture Capital; Diane Dilworth, Chemical Bank; Thomas Schiels, Office of the District Attorney, County of New York; Audrey Twarogowski, Manufacturers & Traders Trust Co.; and Gregory Meredith, Salomon Brothers.

It should go without saying, but it may be nevertheless necessary to add, that none of these individuals, their institutions, or any others bear responsibility for the material and opinions expressed herein. Yet, their support, that has come in many forms and over a long period of time, is and will always be deeply appreciated.

Stephen P. Rappaport
January 1, 1990

Contents

CHAPTER 1

Introduction: What Makes the Affluent Investor Different?

If there is a single thing that so-called how to invest books have not done, it is to focus on a particularly important group of investors, namely, the affluent. These investors have unusual incomes and assets, unique financial needs, and specific feelings about assuming risks that must be taken into account when developing investment strategies that involve a variety of instruments invested under different economic and interest rate scenarios. Furthermore, until now, texts on investments have not made understandable the portfolio management techniques and investment strategies that could be useful to individuals of means. Indeed, it will be shown that investors need not be wedded to investing only, or largely, in a specific type of financial security, such as stocks, government securities, or municipal bonds, excluding others that could be good or even great investments for them.

WHY THE AFFLUENT INVESTOR NEEDS SPECIAL ATTENTION

Each financial security issued or traded in the marketplace has characteristics that are viewed totally differently by each investor, but most especially by the affluent. Whether it is a stock that is of high or low quality, is moving up in price in a potentially stable market, or is moving down in price in an up market, each investor views this security as it relates to his or her own investment strategy or portfolio needs at that point in time. Whether a bond is of high, medium, or low credit quality, has a long- or short-term maturity, or offers a high or low yield in a projected upward or downward interest rate environment, again each investor views this from a unique perspective.

Indeed, each security has its own inherent advantages and disadvantages for purchase or sale, as it relates to the current economic environment and the investor's present status and investment needs. As a result, purchase and sale decisions, based on such factors as changes in market conditions or new credit-quality evaluations, could be applied in different ways for each class of investor, and also for each individual investor.

As a consequence, when the particulars of any given security are not placed within the confines of a market cycle, when they do not focus on an investor's financial needs, when they do not take into account an investor's portfolio strategy, and thus most critically, when they ignore the constraints of a particular group of investors, nothing is learned about how to invest—in what amounts and what quality of securities—and how to make the appropriate alterations in the composition of the investor's portfolio to meet the individual's changing needs and cope with alterations in the conditions of all the financial markets.

Investing, to be sure, is not universal for all individuals. As a group, institutions, corporations, governments, pension funds, mutual funds, and unit trusts differ widely in their own investment parameters and goals and, as a result, in how bond and stock market movements, and those projected, affect their respective holdings and their investment strategies. Individuals, too, are at the mercy of the stock and bond markets, but, perhaps first and last, their investment strategies are most significantly affected by the amount of funds they have to invest—their net assets and their annual incomes. Then, the investment climate, their own risk predilections, and their financial needs and objectives come into play. It occurs in this manner because individual investors can live and function quite well beyond a certain level of assets and income, particularly the affluent.

For the affluent, this does not mean that the larger size of their investable assets actually means less to them or that they should not worry about investment losses. Rather, this concept implies that for the affluent, each bull and bear market requires investment strategies quite different from those employed by small or average investors. Over their life span and during each business cycle, different securities afford the affluent different opportunities for investment, largely because the securities and the environment are, and should be, viewed differently by them.

The concept of looking at securities through the eyes of a particular investor group, such as the affluent, is a way of better fitting the product to the customer. To be sure, not every individual in an investor group, such as those in the category of affluent, will view every financial product and investment decision in the same way. There are also various degrees of affluence, and for every investment decision, there are probably as many individuals. The point, however, is to fine-tune this understanding of a particular investor group to each investor in that group, taking into account the risk postures, income streams, and net worth of each, in order to develop the most appropriate portfolio strategy for each.

WHAT SETS THE AFFLUENT APART FROM OTHER INVESTORS?

What separates the affluent from others is the amount of financial assets they have on hand, or their net income, or some combination of both. Most literature defines affluence as relating to individuals whose incomes are $50,000 or $75,000 a year. However, there is a difference between affluence and affluent investors. Affluent investors have income streams that accumulate in financial portfolios of stocks, bonds, and other investment vehicles. Some or all of the income may have been earned over a short period of time or over a lifetime, or it could have been inherited, and the total amount could run well into the millions. The portfolio size of affluent investors, by definition and for investment strategy purposes, will be defined, categorized, and examined throughout this book. However, it is sufficient to state here that an affluent investor is one whose income and net worth lend themselves to a unique portfolio management concept for investing.

Affluent people very often do not have the time to become deeply involved in the management of their financial portfolios and may not have the knowledge required to participate in the investment process. When affluent investors are familiar with the investment world, often their knowledge is of a small group of stocks or municipal bonds or other financial securities. For most individuals, and even for investment professionals, knowledge of a great variety of investment instruments as well as the ability to manage them over time in line with a specific investment strategy are difficult to acquire and necessitate considerable amounts of time to operationalize with any degree of success. Not surprisingly, the investors least likely to have time available are the affluent, whose taxing jobs often involve a great deal of travel and business-related entertainment. There are only so many hours in a day, and as a result, the affluent have often relegated the management of their investments to a very small proportion of that time and, in some instances, even to others.

As a result, the affluent, despite their financial successes, often find themselves poorly prepared to handle their own financial affairs. Furthermore, the fear of failure in the investment field, an area in which they often have not been appropriately schooled, discourages successful individuals from getting involved in the investment arena. Perhaps this is just a fact of life, but for the affluent, it is a fact that is important to acknowledge and understand.

There are other significant life-style characteristics that affect the ability of affluent individuals to become involved in their investments. For one thing, peer pressure for spending increases as one moves up the economic ladder. Very often these pressures evolve in a single neighborhood, town, or city, but they are characteristic of certain economic groups, regardless of geographic location.

Evidence of this can be seen in advertisements for leisure-related activities, real estate investments, or charity and other fund-raising events, all of which are clearly beyond investors of average means. In other words, one's life-style and its accoutrements are often as important as the total return of one's portfolio, or annual income, or even net worth. This pressure gives rise to episodic needs for capital, usually for purchases, and this affects the affluent investor's financial portfolio by diverting capital away from financial investment and thus affecting a portfolio's return significantly.

Very often the affluents' investment goals are affected by another significant factor—the inheritance of substantial amounts of capital. Sometimes this money comes with strings attached, at least for a specified period of time, for example, the holding of stock in a particular company or honoring requirements for purchase or sale of securities in a trust fund.

More important, however, is one's state of mind about particular investments that are inherited. This could include a bias for specific types of investments such as stocks or bonds or even stocks of particular companies or debt instruments of certain governments or corporations. It may also involve a predisposition for or against the purchase of these kinds of securities. On a broader scale, these predispositions could be more conceptual, relating, for example, to a family member's desire to purchase securities of only the highest quality, such as blue chip stocks or high-quality bonds; or to purchase securities that have short maturities, of one to five years; or to put a substantial amount of one's assets in readily available cash instruments. These notions are often difficult to shed by those who inherit substantial sums, especially if such individuals have been exposed to these investment philosophies over long periods of time and have even come to believe in some of them.

While certain mind-sets do not have to be changed totally—individuals may be comfortable with them, even if they are giving up a larger rate of return on their money—nevertheless, there is certainly room to develop other investment concepts to achieve a diversified portfolio. All these factors greatly impact on the investment objectives of the affluent in a variety of ways. They serve to modify their risk predilections and investment strategies during the different stages of a business cycle and over the course of their lives. Consequently, as a class of investors, the affluent stand strikingly apart from other investors, which makes them select, for purchase and sale, securities in ways that set them apart from other individuals.

WHO ARE THE AFFLUENT INVESTORS?

Mathematically as well as conceptually, it is difficult to define affluent investors, people of means, or those with substantial investable assets and/or income that could place these investors in a category unto themselves. In general, however, affluent investors can establish a portfolio of securities of approximately $50,000 to $100,000, exclusive of their homes and other valuables. Their incomes could be equivalent to the size of their portfolios or even be multiples of it, or vice versa, and include both earned and unearned income and any financial inheritance.

Surely, there are individuals whose financial assets are of such size that they are comparable to those of small- and midsized institutions; these individuals are often in a class apart and require investment services of a specialized variety. However, the portfolio management techniques described here may not necessarily vary for them when compared to other affluent individuals. The same concepts employed for a large portfolio of securities may be applicable to one that is somewhat smaller. What is more important is that these individuals are all clearly beyond the small or average investor in the size of their investable assets and thus demand specialized attention and an individualized investment strategy.

Let us envision a four-tiered grouping of all individual investors by relative wealth levels, according to the size of their assets and their net income. There may be overlap, to be sure, but there are some clear distinctions to be made. In conceptual terms, there is the small, average, upper-middle, and the wealthy individual. As we move down in affluence from the wealthy, the investor is likely to focus less on portfolio management because there are fewer investable funds that can be drawn on to develop a portfolio. Also, more income must be used for general living expenses. There is some level of income, probably at the income range of $60,000 to $100,000 per year for a family of four, depending on where they live, when a portfolio can accrue, but this is not true in every case. Hence, a few of the investment strategies outlined in this book may be useful to this particular investor, but the day-to-day portfolio management concerns may not be apparent.

SOME INVESTMENT CONCEPTS APPLIED TO THE AFFLUENT

For the purposes of this book, the financial assets in which the affluent can invest may be grouped into four general categories: stocks, fixed-income securities (bonds), short-term investment vehicles, and cash. How the investment strategies of these investors are derived and how they approach their portfolios may be strikingly different from how small or average investors go about investing. For instance, affluent investors have, at times, a greater financial capability of assuming risk, however defined, although they may not want to do so. Similarly, affluent investors have a much different perspective for investing at each stage throughout their life cycle. Moreover, the business cycle is characterized by inflationary and recessionary periods and stages of economic growth and contraction—all affecting the direction of the stock and bond markets—which presents investors with substantial funds different problems and opportunities when compared to their smaller investor counterparts.

Most important, from an overall portfolio standpoint, individuals with sizable amounts of disposable funds to invest can do so with greater diversity. They can take larger positions in a greater number of stocks and bonds, they can earn substantially more money in the form of capital appreciation and dividends from stocks and in interest from bonds, and they can move larger amounts of funds into different investments over the total course of a business cycle. This gives rise to a number of concepts that are critical to the management of an affluent individual's financial portfolio. Indeed, the successful movement of even a proportionately small amount of funds, such as from the category of stocks to bonds or from cash to stocks or even among securities within categories, can give rise shortly thereafter to a tremendous relative amount of increased income.

Conversely, incorrect investment decisions can be equally significant for the affluent investor and can cause them to weather losses on a larger scale than the smaller investor. The size of these losses could wipe out most investors but would not necessarily greatly impact the financial viability of affluent ones. Finally, as stock and bond market conditions change, the quicker the affluent investor can transfer funds from one investment to another in the appropriate way, the greater the chance the investor will be able to capture additional returns or even limit losses.

To be sure, affluent investors must be able to allocate appropriately the financial assets in their portfolios and invest strategically both earned and unearned income that continually accrues. The initial allocation of funds to various investments is the first critical step in achieving proportionately greater investment returns. However, as economic and business conditions change, altering the investment composition of the portfolio is absolutely essential to protecting the investor from loss and also to achieving the greatest total return. Reinvesting both earned and unearned income, while taking into account expected market conditions as well as the existing allocation of funds in the portfolio, is equally important.

These are critical portfolio management concepts that must be employed by individuals with substantial funds to invest. To a greater or lesser extent, average investors should look carefully at each of these in the management of their portfolios. However, investors with the most to gain, and also the most to lose, are those with the largest asset bases and income levels. They are a special class of individual investors, and to receive the greatest total return on their investable funds, they must take a strategic approach to the management of their portfolios. This includes the development of an investment strategy that takes into account their specific stage of life, their risk posture, the part of the business cycle within which they are investing, and finally and perhaps most important, the relative attractiveness of the stocks, bonds, and the other investment vehicles available at any given point in time.

WHAT IS A FINANCIAL PORTFOLIO?

This book deals solely with financial securities. It does not address synthetic investment vehicles (such as options and futures), real estate investments, tax planning, or investment funds. Most synthetic investment vehicles are used for hedging, arbitrage, or speculation and seek to take advantage of expected stock or bond market movements or to protect profits or guard against losses. They often entail great risk, are complicated to use, and are therefore employed only by experts or in conjunction with them. Synthetic investment vehicles are usually also an adjunct to the investment process. Often, the investor's stock or bond position is in place before these investment vehicles are employed, or they are employed in conjunction with the purchase of securities. Such vehicles are beyond the scope of this volume.

Although individual investors often purchase packaged products such as mutual funds or unit trusts, investment professionals often advise affluent investors to develop their own portfolios because they have enough funds to engage in the type of diversification generally offered by packaged products. This is not to say that affluent investors should not invest a certain proportion of their financial assets in mutual funds or unit trusts. Those who do not want to construct their own portfolios can certainly benefit from professional management and diversity that funds and other such products offer. However, for the purposes of developing a financial portfolio and engaging in portfolio management, the purchase of packaged products is also beyond the scope of this book.

The tax situations of investors are not dealt with here. Often the last decision that is made in the investment process is a tax one, but that decision may actually be critical in both the short and long run. It is best, therefore, for each investor, affluent or otherwise, to seek the advice of his or her tax advisor, accountant, and attorney before any investment is made. Each case is a specialized one, and the affluent often have substantial needs for attention in this area.

Also, not treated here are direct or participatory investments or ownership interests in partnerships and the like. These are not financial instruments in the classical sense of the term, and therefore they do not fall within the purview of the portfolio strategy concepts developed here for stocks and bonds. Similarly, commodities, such as copper, gold, cotton, or coffee, are also not financial vehicles. In addition, their trading activity often employs the use of synthetic investment vehicles such as options and futures. Also, commodities are traded in highly specialized markets where participation requires great professional expertise. As a result, an in-depth knowledge of these investments is critical for their successful use. More often than not, individual investors are relatively unfamiliar with these vehicles, and they are advised to seek professional expertise when dealing with them. Commodity trading also involves great risk.

The point here is that the portfolio strategies developed in this book are for those who perhaps could use them to a greater extent than others—the affluent investors—and the focus of this study is on their overall financial portfolios of stocks, fixed-income securities or bonds, short-term investments, and cash vehicles.

PART 1

The Investment World of the Affluent Investor

CHAPTER 2

Investment Life Cycles of the Affluent Investor

It is generally true that over the course of time, the types of investments that are appropriate for individual investors change as the years progress. The financial investments change in kind and quality, among other ways, and, in most instances, this evolution is a function of the different financial situations in which individuals often find themselves from their first years of work through retirement. Moreover, there are some sharp distinctions between the life cycle of the average investor and that of the more affluent one. Also related to this concept is the change in the amount of risk investors are willing to assume as they grow older. As a result, the affluent investor's risk perceptions during the different stages of his or her life cycle may be strikingly different from those of the smaller investor, and thus the investment decisions of an affluent individual over the course of his or her lifetime may be substantially different from decisions of others in the marketplace.

A TYPICAL INVESTMENT LIFE CYCLE OF THE AVERAGE INVESTOR

The investment life cycle of the typical investor is usually divided into three age groups. From the time an individual starts work through about the age of 45 or so, most investors believe that they can take their most risk-prone posture to investing, and it is during these years that they are most likely to invest in securities that carry somewhat higher risks but also have the potential for greater returns. Normally, these investments include stocks that offer a greater than average chance of price appreciation relative to the stock market as a whole and thus the opportunity for quicker than average capital gains. Investors may look for higher-yielding bonds that might be of slightly lower credit quality and may trade them more actively than would be the case for more conservative investors or those utilizing investment strategies in the later years of their lives.

The second phase of an investor's life cycle might be considered as running from the mid-40s through approximately age 60. This is usually the time when family responsibilities are the heaviest, and there is often the need to fund the expense of the children's college education and the mortgage on one's home as well as pay the day-to-day costs of living and providing for a growing family. During this rather protracted period of responsibility, most investors, and perhaps rightly so, tend to seek investments that afford them an above-average current income either through stock dividends or interest earned on bonds. Investors may also want to increase the quality of their investments by seeking stocks that may provide some chance of sound growth but also represent quality, while looking for bonds of good quality that have little chance of default.

After the age of about 60, investors try to preserve their capital more than in any other period in their investment life cycle. They tend to concentrate on living off the income generated by their principal, but they also are seeking to assume much less risk. As a result, when they purchase stocks, they usually seek shares in those companies that are considered to be of highest quality; similar considerations go into the selection of bonds. In addition, although seeking current income is an important conservative aspect of their investment strategy, at this stage of their lives, they also purchase bonds that have shorter maturities, thus providing the opportunity for having the principal amount of their money come due much quicker, reinvesting that principal very soon thereafter.

This is a typical, albeit simplistic, view of the investment life cycle of the typical or average investor. The stages are characterized not only by age segment and perspective on investment strategy, but also by the overall risk perspective that settles on their investment strategies and molds the selection of their securities for purchase and/or sale. To be sure, the investment life cycle of the small or average investor has, as its underpinning, a type of inertia, and that is reflected in a concern for the maintenance of principal and the fear of loss of that principal throughout their lives, especially in light of the financial responsibilities that beset most people.

THE FIVE INVESTMENT LIFE-CYCLE STAGES OF THE AFFLUENT

The stages of affluent investors' investment life cycles derive as much from a perception of economic and market reality as they do from their financial wherewithal over the course of their lifetime. This is so because the affluent investors must first approach their investments from a portfolio strategy point of view. Their stages of life are compressed into shorter but better delineated ones with somewhat differing financial needs and the life expectancy of most individuals has increased greatly, both have been very important for the investment strategies of the affluent in particular.

Each segment of an affluent investor's life cycle is described in this section, after which an appropriate risk posture for that individual at that stage of the investor's life cycle is offered.

Throughout these discussions, certain episodic needs for capital will be highlighted as will the inherent tension between what these financial requirements are and what the affluent investor's own spending habits have become, which, to a greater or lesser degree, may drain the potential financial portfolio or impact the investment strategies that go into the management of it.

The Sky's the Limit: Ages 25 to 35

This is the first stage in the life cycle of the affluent investor, and it usually occurs in the postschooling years beginning with the individual's first major full-time employment. Even with a small amount of inherited funds or none at all, young, potentially affluent, individual investors usually begin to accrue large amounts of funds as a result of, for instance, the relatively high-paying employment in metropolitan areas. Their mind-sets often anticipate an endless, increasingly upward, spiral of income that they believe is commensurate with the long hours required of their financially rewarding jobs. Such employment may culminate in a partnership or a senior executive position within a firm. It is these early years, in many cases, that separate the affluent investor from the average investor.

The period begins when all the initial financial needs of these individuals appear to have been met. A steep increase in income usually occurs during the first few years of employment, but the investment strategy of these individuals is usually constrained by their need or desire to use their newly found affluence to purchase a home or a fine car or perhaps start a family. Funds may accrue, but not enough time is available to develop a portfolio strategy. This period is often coupled with an inherent feeling that the increasing amounts of money accruing from earned income can continue, and this is reflected in the individuals' spending habits. In addition, there is often a lack of knowledge and experience in investing on the part of these individuals who are in the incipient stages of affluence.

All these factors converge on an individual's strategy at this early stage of his or her working life. They mitigate what might be a more risk-averse investment posture or a far too aggressive investment strategy; they often, to be sure, go too far to the investment extremes. It is especially important for the affluent investor to begin developing an investment strategy and financial portfolio in the later years of this first stage of the investment life cycle.

The Consolidation of Expectations: Ages 36 to 45

It is in this stage that the affluent individual begins to come to grips with the possibility that his or her personal income will not continue to increase at the previous rate. At the same time, the individual faces the expenditures associated with raising a family, educating children, and paying for housing. In the later phase of this stage, many of the major expenditures are out of the way, and the investor can begin to concentrate, to a greater extent, on portfolio management and investment strategy. To be sure, the affluent investor's financial portfolio may have grown enormously during this period as tremendous amounts of annual income continue to accrue, but for many, this will not be the case. It happens only if and when a business is sold during this period or the individual rises quickly up the corporate or partnership ladder, where annual income increases can even exceed those of the first stage and thus result in a substantially larger portfolio.

In later years, there may be a concern for the loss of principal as a result of the investor's weathering a few problematic business cycles and perhaps seeing the stock market plummet. These situations could have occurred in the early years of an affluent investor's life cycle, but during those times, they may not have had the kind of depressing effect that their recollection or their actuality does now, and this affects an affluent investor's investment strategy. Previously, responsibilities were not as great, anticipatory income was potentially large, and expenses were relatively slim.

During this phase, the affluent investor's mind-set is also greatly impacted by a "live now" syndrome. Specifically, if investors and their families do not use their financial assets to make the purchases, take the vacations, buy the real estate, and live the life-styles for which they had hoped, they may not be able to have these luxuries later on, or if they can afford them, they may not be able to truly enjoy them. This has the potential of causing the affluent to spend greatly, thus diluting the financial portfolio, or making the affluent investor invest too aggressively to maximize income or too conservatively to limit risk, while spending some principal. As a result, for the affluent investor, this is perhaps the most complex and trying stage of his or her investment life cycle, and it comes in the wake of a period in which not much attention was paid to appropriate portfolio management techniques and long-range investment strategy.

Stepping Out: Ages 46 to 55

Although the consolidation of financial assets, the move to limit speculation, and the concentration on income-producing investments usually typifies this age for average investors in an effort to conserve principal and prepare for retirement, this may not be so for the affluent investor. This investor usually reaches historically high levels of income and asset accumulation during these years, especially if and when inheritance rears its bitter-sweet head. More conservative investment and financial planning often overtakes most average investors during this period when the largest amount of their expenditures have taken place for family, housing, and the children's education. For the affluent, however, this can be the period of greatest growth potential and should be the most significant time for their concentration on the management of their portfolios and the development of invest-ment strategies. Their basic needs have already been met, a level of acceptable expenditures has been reached, and for most, it is difficult to either slow down dramatically or increase consistently and measurably the amount of money outflow.

The reallocation of funds in their portfolios and the rede-ployment of earned and unearned income into appropriate invest-ments are critical activities at this time, especially considering the fact that large sums of money may become available when real estate investments are liquidated. At this time, the affluent must concentrate on maximizing investment returns whether they believe (1) that money and increased rate of return may really not be that necessary, or important, or (2) that the process of achieving those ends takes too much time, or it is better left totally to others. This situation is most likely to occur when the affluent investors' extremely demanding and high-visibility jobs to which they have ascended take precedence, in pride and prestige, over their personal financial portfolio.

Toning Down: Ages 56 to 65

The early part of this stage, for most other investors, is one that results in a consolidation of assets, an accent on the preservation of capital, and the purchase of income-oriented investments, all in preparation of retirement. For the affluent, however, this stage is markedly different in substance and style. Affluent investors often reach an exalted professional position that comes with either increased pressure or a relatively comfortable responsibility level, both of which have, as their by-product, the accrual of additional income, often in large amounts.

A movement to a more conservative investment posture is likely, but active portfolio management with a thoughtful investment strategy often occurs to a greater extent here because it has been postponed up until this point. Concentration on a less aggressive investment posture is appropriate at this time. Usually, most average investors divest themselves of fixed-income securities with long-term maturities and of growth-oriented stocks. Affluent investors, however, can keep a fairly decent proportion of their portfolio funds in these financial vehicles. The problem, at this point in time, is that large amounts of interest and dividends are coming in as is principal that is due, so that the deployment of this unearned income must be done with a tremendous amount of forethought. Also, the affluent investors' relatively large gross incomes make the allocation of net income to appropriate portfolio investments particularly critical, especially when expenses have usually abated to a large degree.

Retirement and Beyond: Age 66 Plus

For the small and average investor, this stage is normally characterized by the consolidation of their portfolio accompanied by an attempt to live off a fixed income with preservation of principal as a critical aspect of their investment strategy, especially as life expectancy continues to increase. This is often not so for the affluent investors. They can dip into their principal, usually without any real appreciable problem in the years ahead, but they are also the least likely to have to go into principal for living expenses and the like.

As a result, the investment opportunities for the affluent at this stage loom large for greatly increasing their total rate of return. Consequently, portfolio management can become an interesting avocation, especially because total retirement is often not the case for the affluent, and consultancies, retainers, private business ventures, and all sorts of work-related possibilities are important, if not, dominant life-style factors. Therefore, the goals of moderate portfolio growth and above-average rate of return are still seen as important to the investment strategy, if not for the older affluent investors themselves, but certainly for their heirs.

CHAPTER 3

Investment Risks
and the Affluent Investor

Perhaps the most significant factor affecting an individual's investment strategy is his or her willingness to assume risk when there is a desire to achieve greater returns. This concept is especially important to understand and operationalize effectively by those who have a large amount of funds to invest and therefore a substantial amount to gain or to lose in the investment process. In the most general terms, individual investors come to the investment process with certain preconceived notions about their own willingness to assume risk, to greater or lesser degrees, and thus reap proportionately larger or smaller investment returns. To be sure, this notion can be broken down into an individual's feelings about the riskiness of stocks versus bonds and the willingness to assume more or less risk during different economic cycles and different points in their lives. However, to understand better an individual's risk posture, especially the posture of the affluent investor, it is exceedingly important to deal with the concept of risk in its varying degrees of intensity and then to relate it to specific investment vehicles and circumstances.

THE CATEGORIES OF RISK

From a conceptual standpoint, most individuals would agree that there are three general broad categories of risk, and that they, as individuals, can be accorded one of these three positionings, namely, conservative, average, or aggressive. However, these designations present some philosophical difficulties to those who would eventually be placed in one of them. Most people, for instance, would not like to believe that they are aggressive. The use of the word "aggressive" as applied to today's investment world often relates to the individual who engages in speculative activities. These activities are usually shunned by most investors, and perhaps surprisingly, affluent individuals usually steer clear of many speculative types of investments.

Many individuals also do not like to think of themselves as "average" in risk perception or in anything else. They believe that they can differentiate themselves from other individuals in a whole variety of areas, perhaps even viewing themselves as special in some sense, and thus able to take advantage of inefficiencies in the marketplace. Although they might not see themselves as being aggressive or even conservative, they certainly do not believe that they are average—at least most people do not. Furthermore, while many investors and individuals who do not engage in investing may, at times, view themselves and their investment posture as being "conservative," they would not characterize themselves as totally in that class. As a conservative investor, they believe, and perhaps rightly so, that they would be adopting an unnecessarily conservative risk posture, and thus sacrificing substantial investment returns on their financial assets.

As a result of this assessment of the three general risk categories, analysts and investors often break these categories down into seven subgroups, in which it may be easier to place individuals in terms of their risk posture. These categories, ranging from risk averse to risk prone, may be termed ultraconservative, conservative, moderately conservative, moderate or average, moderately aggressive, aggressive, and speculative. In this nomenclature, for example, the moderately aggressive category attributes to the investor a desire and ability to assume slightly more risk than the average investor but not to be aggressive or invest in speculative investments to any great degree. It involves seeking gains, being moderately assertive in this process, being sensible about taking risks, seeking a competitive advantage in the marketplace, but being reasonably restrained from adopting a truly aggressive posture with all the problems that it would normally entail. Putting one's money in aggressive investments for an overall risk posture of an entire portfolio may be appropriate for certain individuals some of the time. For most individuals, however, it may not fully express their desire to conserve their principal and financial assets while assuming the degree of risk necessary to reap larger returns.

Most important, levels of risk can in fact run the entire gamut of categories suggested, but many affluent investors can adopt an above-average risk posture to reap the increased incremental returns necessary to outperform the market but not to assume such risk that they may lose capital. This posture certainly may not be appropriate for all affluent investors all of the time and for stocks as well as bonds, but it will develop in the affluent investor a mind-set toward investing that will ultimately help to create an investment strategy appropriate for his or her portfolio.

INVESTMENT RISK IN STOCKS AND BONDS

As a concept, risk is understandable, but when applied to stocks versus bonds, it has a much different connotation. This is especially important in the case of the affluent investor who may invest in a larger number of different stocks and fixed-income securities with widely different potential rates of return. The most basic difference is that a stock investment is subject to market movements in price and has no maturity or time when an individual usually receives back the full amount invested. However, in the case of fixed-income securities or bonds, an individual invests a certain amount of money and the principal is returned when the investment matures, and over the course of the investment's life, the individual investor receives a stated rate of return or interest income.

Ultimately when dealing with the term "risk," investors are usually concerned about the loss of principal, that is, loss of the amount of money invested. In the stock market, one can theoretically lose the total amount invested—if the stock price drops to zero. However, bonds are redeemed at maturity, so the entire principal amount is repaid to the investor. If the investor sells the bonds before they mature, and interest rates have risen, prices on the bonds will drop so that there is a possible loss of principal on the sale. If the bond defaults as a result of financial pressures or the like on the issuing entity, the bond investor may lose the total amount invested, but this is unlikely because, even in bankruptcy, a certain amount of principal is often provided to the investors in the form of compensation for their investments. In these instances, therefore, the possibility of losing one's entire investment in bonds is remote.

There are some other conceptual problems relating to the loss of principal by investing in bonds. These include such instances when the bonds are called or redeemed before they mature at a price that is less than the price at which the bonds are trading so that the investor loses money on paper. Such problems, however, pale next to the potential loss possible when investing in stocks. The basic difference is that stocks lack the maturity that there is on bonds, which is the time when the investors can receive all of their investment back. In other words, a stock can drop in value and never return to the price level at which it was purchased. In addition, the individual investor usually counts on a certain amount of dividend income from the stock as well as possible appreciation in the price of the stock over time, either or both of which are not guaranteed. It is worth noting that the eventual rate of return over very long periods is higher in equity investments than in fixed-income securities. However, individuals invest, assume risks, have income needs, and are willing to adjust their portfolios within much shorter time frames such as the maturities on fixed-income investments (i.e., a period of up to 30 years).

Another key problem not usually focused on when defining risk vis-à-vis stocks and bonds is that stock market movements may affect different stock groups and different stocks within each group much differently. Price movements in the bond market, however, come largely as a result of the changes in interest rates and usually affect bonds of all kinds in the same general way. Only rarely in interest rate–sensitive markets, such as the bond market, do different sectors of bonds or different bonds in particular move in opposite directions to one another, with large differences in price. Spread differentials may increase or decrease, but the prices of the securities do not move in opposite directions most of the time. As contrasted with bonds, this imbues the stock market, and stocks in particular, with a degree of incalculable risk that makes it difficult to select stocks all the time that will appreciate in price as a result of expectations about stock and stock market movements.

Obviously, this provides as many problems as it does opportunities for investors. However, it appears to offer more problems for those who must fear the worst and thus hedge their investments or get out of the market, if necessary, and these are more likely to be smaller investors. Yet these scenarios afford more opportunities for greater capital appreciation if the market moves up for those who can weather economic downturns or who can allocate a greater proportion of their investable assets to more growth-oriented investments. This naturally applies to individuals with more relative wealth, namely, affluent investors.

As a result of this conceptual view of risk and return in stocks and bonds, it is important for investors to adopt a risk profile for each group of investments individually and for both groups taken together. For the affluent investor, this is especially critical because of the amount of income that could ultimately be garnered by appropriate investing as well as the risk that could be taken that may result in an overall gains or losses for the portfolio taken as a whole or for different segments of the portfolio individually.

CHANGES IN RISK POSTURE FOR STOCKS AND BONDS

Changes in an individual investor's risk posture can occur for either stocks or bonds or both or the portfolio as a whole and be altered by the amount of funds that the investor has allocated to each category of assets and by which securities are purchased in each category. (These differences in how a risk posture is altered will be explained further by examples throughout this book.) A conceptual problem arises, however, when the affluent or other investor groups embark on a program to structure their portfolio or purchase securities in ways that attempt to take advantage of many investment opportunities at once. This may subject the investor to such increased risk vis-à-vis the expected return that it substantially changes the risk posture of the individual's portfolio. Furthermore, and most important, it may move the investor into a posture that may be more aptly characterized by the next greatest risk level. For instance, structuring a portfolio to take advantage of a wide variety of opportunities for market upside, with the appropriately attendant risk, could move an investor from a profile of moderately aggressive to truly aggressive and thus thrust the investor into a risk profile that was initially unanticipated.

For a particular market or a specific part of the business cycle, investors might want to, and indeed have to, modify their risk exposure slightly, adopting a more aggressive or conservative stance. In such a case, however, the investor does so knowingly, and it may not entail such a significant movement to a different risk posture that it alters the entire risk position of the portfolio. This change is usually accompanied by changing investments in stocks or bonds or both to take advantage of market opportunities and employing all the possible financial investments to take advantage of the market's potential movement.

During changes in the business cycle and as a result of movements in the stock and bond markets, changes in a moderately aggressive risk posture are likely to occur, but this is much more likely to be so for the small or average investor than the affluent one. Average investors seem to be in and out of the market in greater numbers and for more reasons than the affluent who are usually in the market because of the sheer size of their financial assets or for lack of other vehicles in which to invest. Even after the stock market crash of October 19, 1987, a tremendous number of small investors left the stock market for a long time and many simply did not return. It is likely that, of the smaller investors who did remain in the market, their risk posture was reduced enormously, both in the kinds of stocks they purchased and their movement into purchases of fixed-income vehicles, although there is no way to quantify this.

Contrarily, institutions and some wealthy investors did some "bottom fishing" in the wake of this crash, purchasing stocks they considered to be bargains, so that while they may have changed their own risk posture, the change was not as great as that of small or average investors. Smaller investors are also more likely to jump on the bandwagon during wild stock market upswings, at least in greater proportionate numbers, than are affluent investors, perhaps because not as large a percentage was originally in the market. As a result, the risk posture of the smaller investor could be changed markedly.

In addition, the affluent investor can better weather the volatility associated with stages of a business cycle, while at the same time reaping larger rates of return on much more substantial amounts of principal invested. Consequently, for a larger amount invested by the affluent investor and the larger rate of return associated with this, the affluent investor can earn increasingly greater rates of return than can the smaller investor who, perhaps of necessity, might have to adopt a more risk-averse posture.

CHAPTER 4

The Business Cycle
and the Affluent Investor

The stock and bond markets are greatly affected by the natural cycle of business activity that comes as a result of changes in economic conditions, and there is perhaps no other individual investor who is so well equipped to take advantage of opportunities afforded by the cyclical nature of the economy than the affluent investor. Indeed, periods of economic expansion and contractions as well as inflation and recessions cause stock prices to rise or fall and interest rates to increase or decrease. The cycles and their stages can be lengthy or short in duration, can be extremely volatile or relatively placid, can result in stock prices climbing while interest rates are declining, and vice versa, move in tandem, or can occur quickly or slowly. Through all these situations, individual investors with the largest funds on hand can structure their portfolios to take advantage of market upswings and perhaps limit losses to the greatest extent. They are also the investors who stand to lose the most in terms of total rate of return on their portfolios.

AN OVERVIEW OF THE BUSINESS CYCLE

The basic business cycle can be characterized by six stages: growth, peak, contraction, recession, trough, and expansion. It is generally agreed that the expansionary periods may last somewhat longer than those periods characterized by contraction. Expansions run from one to seven years or so whereas contractions last from approximately six months to five years. In general, the entire cycle may last a number of years and can vary in the extent to which the ups and downs are severe or mild, highly volatile or relatively smooth. Economic indicators are usually employed to discern the stages of the business or economic cycle and the extent to which they are severe. The most notable one is the gross national product (GNP) provided by the U.S. Department of Commerce and purported to represent the dollar or market value of all goods and services produced by the country during a single year. When the economy is expanding, the GNP rises at a rate above or faster than its historic trend, and when the economy is contracting, the GNP tends to fall accordingly. The "industrial production index" is another measure that is used in much the same way. Both these numbers, when reported, can cause fluctuations in the general prices of stocks and can also affect interest rates.

These parts of the business cycle fuel, to a greater or lesser extent, inflationary pressures. Inflation, usually measured by the GNP deflator, indicates a general increase in prices of goods and services. Hyperinflation causes quick and large price increases over relatively short periods of time. Disinflation is a slower inflation rate. And deflation is generally associated with falling prices. A recession normally occurs when the economy has failed to grow for about two quarters or so. When recessions become severe, they are called depressions, and these can last for relatively long periods of time.

The economic cycle and its stages greatly affect the stock and bond markets, in part by impacting interest rates that cause price movements in both markets. This has implications for investors, particularly those with substantial assets. Stock prices are generally expected to increase as the economy expands and decrease as the economy contracts and moves toward a recession. Yet stock price movements can be anticipatory, because they often begin moving downward before the business cycle peaks and the expansionary period comes to a close. Similarly, stock prices begin moving upward before the economic expansion begins anew. Bond prices generally decrease as the economy expands and inflationary pressures increase bond yields during that time although this is not always so.

As the economy begins to contract and head into the recessionary stage, interest rates usually drop measurably, but this has not always been so. Over the last 20 years, interest rates have been relatively high during inflationary and also deflationary times, but not necessarily as high as they have been during inflation.

THE AFFLUENT AND CONSENSUS INVESTING

Understanding how the economy and the business cycle affect bond yields and stock market prices, and then forecasting bond market and stock market movements, is a critical activity for all investors, especially for the affluent, but it is almost impossible to do. What is interesting is that few, if any, professionals have a stellar track record in this type of forecasting. Furthermore, few investors have developed conceptual models in their own mind about how and when these events could occur, and, from a personal standpoint, perhaps no one has more to gain or to lose than the affluent investor. For deciding which securities to purchase, for developing investment strategies, and for managing portfolios, the understanding of how business cycles affect the markets is critical, but it is difficult at best to make consistently accurate market predictions as a consequence. Fine-tuning one's projections is even more difficult, because the speed with which these markets move and their volatility often outpaces even the predictive ability of professionals. It makes the task a virtual impossibility for almost anyone, although a few market prognosticators may be correct once in a while.

As a result, it is important that the affluent adopt what might be termed a "risk-modifying" strategy in developing their expectations and projections about stock and bond market movements. The strategy suggested here is to take the markets' bearings every three months and not become involved in studying the daily numbers that could move the market sharply within a day or two but not mean much over the long haul. Quarterly adjustments are much more likely to give a smoother picture of the market and lower the risks of overcompensating on a short-term basis. Moreover, taking an average of the most widely followed economists and stock market analysts so that every quarter, an investor's predictive deviations are not very wide of what might be projected as overall targets of where the markets are expected to be over the near to midterm, eliminates doing a substantial amount of work independently and precludes forcing the affluent investor into a different risk posture by overcompensating based on incorrect expectations. (Of course, investors may have their own favorite economist and stock analysts and may prefer to follow their projections and recommendations.)

INVESTING WITHIN THE TIME DIMENSION OF ECONOMIC CYCLES

Economic cycles have a time dimension—that is, they have a beginning, a middle, and an end. Each stage of the cycle also has a beginning, a middle, and an end, but the length of time for each stage within a cycle and for the cycle as a whole is unpredictable, although generally, as noted earlier, even the longest cycles do not last more than a few years. As a result, an individual develops a level of confidence about when each stage, within the cycle, is likely to end, and the next one begin, and the extent to which each part of the cycle is volatile or will likely result in large market upswings or downswings. This must be understood because individual investors are making decisions about their own investment strategy by taking into account, first, the direction of the economy on a quarterly basis or so and, then, allocating, in the most general sense, their resources on that basis with certain degrees of confidence.

Because the whole cycle has a beginning and an end and so do the cycles' stages, they have time dimensions. The longer investors wait to take actions and restructure their portfolios in anticipation of the next stage of the cycle, the more likely it is that the stage will end sooner rather than later. Getting past the initial and intermediate parts of the stage (i.e., the first group of quarters) is the real test of holding to one's own investment strategy without restructuring the portfolio, and thus possibly losing the opportunity for garnering greater total returns over the long term. While there may be great volatility within any stage of the cycle, there is also the possibility that the stage will end abruptly and, for instance, stock prices may plummet or rise quickly, or bond prices may fall or rise as yields go up or down. This tends to force smaller investors toward a principal-conserving strategy in an effort to protect the money they have invested against losses. Smaller investors may, therefore, more actively restructure their portfolios or their investments on a quarterly basis while the affluent has the ability to "hang in there longer" within each stage of the cycle. Some quarterly portfolio modifications may be made by affluent investors as a result of widely volatile markets and a loss of confidence in some of their expectations, while holding to their general investment strategy and not liquidating, to any significant degree, their present investments.

VOLATILITY, THE INTERNATIONAL MARKETS, AND THE AFFLUENT INVESTOR

As noted earlier, until the mid-1970s, economic cycles were fairly predictable in terms of their effect on the direction of the stock and bond market movements; since then, however, they have become much less so and somewhat more volatile. This has been coupled with a generally ratcheting up of interest rates from about 5 percent to as high as 21 percent from the 1950s to the early 1980s and an upswing in stock prices from approximately

500 to as high as 2700, as measured by the Dow Jones Industrial Average. This activity has been accompanied by great volatility of bond and stock market prices, sometimes on a daily basis. Some would argue, however, that many countries have inflation rates that are multiples of what the United States experienced in the early 1980s and have similar situations with regard to stock market prices.

Yet, for the U.S. economy, there may be something strikingly different about the preceding levels that may not be sustainable over long periods of time. For one thing, credit at around 20 percent is very expensive, individuals as well as institutions shirk from paying such high interest rates, and the government becomes extremely concerned when interest rates reach this level. On the stock market side, the recent high levels of earnings multiples reflected in stock prices is a situation that some believe is unsustainable, especially with such high stock market volume. Still, some others believe that the stock market could go increasingly higher.

To be sure, there may be certain unrelated reasons beyond the simple fundamental ones of economics and company earnings that are at work here. One possibility is the international dimension that has taken hold on the American economy, making it a much more global one. It is now more homogeneous and more affected by worldwide events as is the world economy by the U.S. trade deficit and budget imbalance. This has given rise to great volatility in bond and stock market prices. Some challenged estimates indicate that, in each of these markets, volatility has increased four to five times more than it was five to ten years ago, largely as a result of the newer international dimension.

As a result of this and coupled with the use of synthetic investment vehicles such as options, futures, portfolio insurance, and the like, the generally larger swings in the market are to be expected. Whatever the case, this volatility, and the effect of the international markets on the U.S. economy and its stock and bond markets has great impact on all investors, particularly the affluent. It makes it more difficult for investors to stick to their investment goals and strategies, largely because the precipitous ups and downs of the markets put emotional pressure on investors to change their investment policies and risk postures and, thus, to coin a phrase, to "go with the flow," even when the "flow" is just a result of short-term volatility within a particular stage of an overall market cycle.

For the affluent, however, this situation provides great opportunities as well as great risks. Perhaps most important, this volatility widens greatly the differences in likely investment strategies and resultant stock and bond purchases between the affluent and the average investor. The smaller investor, as noted earlier, is likely to withdraw more quickly, recoiling from either bond or stock market purchases in larger numbers than the affluent and also stay away from the markets in the face of seemingly, though not necessarily, problematic conditions.

Also, markets today are more international in size, scope, and substance and, on any given day, may be more affected by the trade deficit figures than any other number. This is useful information for the professional traders who are buying and selling blocks of securities and who are trading on expected or anticipated rates of inflation and interest rates, and also resultant stock and bond prices, even if their expectations turn out to be incorrect. Affluent investors, however, should set their goals on investing based on quarterly trends, adopting a middle ground that should parallel consensus predictions made by economists about interest rates and stock market analysts on stock prices.

PART 2

The Affluent Investor's Stock Market Investments

CHAPTER 5

Stock Selection for the Affluent Investor

More than any other investor in the marketplace, the affluent investor has the ability and the financial resources to take advantage of the tremendous opportunities for gain by purchasing stocks; conversely, this investor is also subject to great pitfalls and thus substantial losses connected with increased risk. In other words, affluent investors can capture increased total returns on their portfolios by investing in the stock market, at the expense of exposure to the greater risks normally associated with volatile markets.

HOW IS STOCK SELECTION DIFFERENT?

Analysts, investment advisors, account managers, and investment strategists throughout the financial community inundate investors with information about what each considers to be the most appropriate investments in particular stocks at any given point in time. Each claims that, for the risks involved, their particular stock recommendations are likely to have the greatest chance of capital appreciation or increased total return. There is often great diversity in their recommendations. For instance, some tout large-dividend-paying stocks, others suggest blue chip stocks, and some argue that stocks with low price-to-earnings multiples are appropriate investments. Obviously, any investor cannot buy all these stocks all the time, and very often these recommendations are quickly changed.

On a more fundamental level, however, there is even great diversity in analysts' projections for the direction that the stock market is expected to go and the rate of speed at which this movement might occur. Stock selection is one problem, but discerning whether the market is going to move up or down or stabilize is surely a more basic concern. The answer affects all stocks, but there is often very little agreement about the stock market's direction, and, perhaps, it is impossible that there be so. All this affects the individual investor's capability of structuring the stock portion of his or her portfolio and, for investors with substantial funds, these situations must be looked at with great care.

In addition, affluent investors are more likely to develop greater exactitude in purchasing strategies. For instance, they may purchase certain stocks and hold them for a short period of time, such as for three to six months, or hold them for much longer. They may also purchase different amounts of the same stock at slower or quicker paces depending on expectations about the movement of the market as a whole, a particular group of stocks, or a particular stock specifically. This all gives rise for the need to develop a method of stock selection by those individuals who are most likely to make the largest purchases of the greatest number of stocks.

It follows also that the larger and more diversified a portfolio is, the more complicated are the concepts involved in the management of it. This includes the reinvestment of funds after the sale of stocks into purchases of other stocks that are already owned in the portfolio or new stocks that had as yet not been purchased. The amount of funds that are reinvested is likely to be strikingly greater for the affluent investor than it is for the small or average one. Furthermore, the affluent investor is much more likely to have a consistently larger amount of unearned and earned income available to invest in the stock section of the portfolio. Consequently, an understanding of stock market strategies and stock fundamentals of companies for a wider range of stocks is likely to be a more important consideration when developing an overall investment plan. Finally, and perhaps most important, the larger stock purchaser should have a better understanding of the industry and product life cycles of the companies issuing stock.

RISKS AND REWARDS IN THE STOCK MARKET

From a risk-reward standpoint, it is the affluent investor who has the most to gain or to lose from increases or decreases in the prices of stocks that are purchased. This stems partly from the fact that stocks generally have wider price swings than do bonds. Thus, if an individual investor purchases stocks and bonds for a total of $1000 each, the stocks could move up to $1300 or drop to $700 over a relatively short period of time whereas a bond will likely never increase 30 percent or drop 30 percent in value during its entire life, through to maturity. In addition, stocks, unlike bonds, lack a fixed maturity that virtually guarantees investors the full value of their investment at that point in time, as noted earlier.

This also means that an individual investor with more funds to live on and to invest may be better able to weather market volatility on a daily, monthly, or yearly basis during long economic downturns when the price of the stocks purchased are depressed than can a small or average investor.

Even with wild swings in the stock market now seen as the norm, greater gains may still be achieved by investing in stocks over the long term. Of the many studies comparing the total rate of return on stocks and bonds over time, a great number of these suggest that over the long haul, stocks are the better investment. This assumes, however, that the individual investor can withstand the downside if prices on the stocks purchased drop and remain there for a relatively long period of time or if the market is especially volatile. Even so, it is the affluent investor who has the greatest financial assets available so as to reap the greatest gains when the stock market moves up but also has the largest amount of funds to lose in the complicated process of investing in stocks.

UNDERSTANDING THE STOCK SELECTION PROCESS

There may be as many ways to evaluate and analyze the stocks of companies as there are analysts and investors. Each may focus on different aspects of the company, its stock, or the market as a whole and weigh each of the myriad characteristics somewhat differently, thus eliciting a different selection as the most appropriate stock to purchase at any given point in time. It logically follows then that not every analyst can always be right about each stock that he or she selects as one for purchase or sale. There is a tremendous amount of data to understand and digest, and there are thousands of professionals who engage in this activity for their livelihoods.

Yet it is not clear that any individual, analyst, or investor has had consistent success in selecting all stocks that always yield the greatest return over a given time period for a given level of risk. Even more important is that the purchase of any particular stock that produces appreciably greater gains than those that could be achieved by purchasing stocks replicating the general market may not be an appropriate purchase for all individual investors. The most significant aspect of this evaluation, however, is that a tremendous amount of material must be assimilated when purchasing stocks, and few individuals have developed a paradigmatic method for dealing with the vast array of data about the market in general and stocks in particular. Nevertheless, it is critical to have a general grasp of these concepts and also to create some method with which to deal with the large amount of available data. It is even more important for an affluent investor to engage in this activity than it is for a smaller one because of the size of the affluent investor's financial assets that could be used to purchase stocks in large numbers and amounts.

The development of an ability to select stocks for purchase will not likely result in the individual investor's becoming incredibly conversant in all the areas of stock analysis, nor is it appropriate that the investor spend countless hours performing the stock selection task. The mind-set that must be developed by the investor, particularly the affluent one, is more a total understanding of how the basic analytical areas fit together in the stock selection process.

For affluent investors, the point of the stock selection process, and perhaps more important, of the development of it, is to find the easiest way to understand what is and is not important to take into account when selecting stocks. This includes the appropriate questions to ask that will elicit information about the particular stock in question, and the industry group and subgroup into which it best fits, while allowing the affluent investor to provide some significant input about stock selection when structuring the stock portion of the portfolio. All this is designed to be accomplished in the shortest period of time possible.

The process may seem simple enough, but with all the available data about the economy, the stock market, industry groups and subgroups, as well as particular stocks, the process is as complex as it is critical. However, for those individuals who invest large sums of money in the stock market and who need diversification, this process is a critical one.

WHEN TO INVEST IN THE STOCK MARKET

Structuring a portfolio or portion of one composed of stocks inevitably involves three important decisions. The first is whether or not to invest in the stock market; the second is the extent to which one should invest as an overall proportion of an individual's total portfolio; and the third involves how to select particular stocks in which to invest. All these decisions are particularly important to affluent investors who, by virtue of the size of their investable assets, may desire to have a substantial amount of funds invested in a diversified selection of stocks even if the total amount invested in these securities may only be a small proportion of the investors' total portfolio.

There are two principal ways to analyze the relative attractiveness of the stock market in general and of specific stocks in particular: fundamental or technical. The problem of predicting stock market movements is much the same as the problem of predicting the course of interest rates. In the case of interest rates, it is often best to rely on the expertise of economists who are professionals at this task—and to select the average prediction of all well-known economists and then make some determination as to the relative likelihood of this average occurring.

Much the same can be done in evaluating the stock market. Professional investment strategists make determinations of how overvalued or undervalued the stock market is at any given point in time based on a wealth of data available that has been finely tuned with their own computer programs and their own perspectives. Professionals also take into account what is more commonly termed the technical aspects of the stock market. These include such wide-ranging characteristics as the movement of selected market indexes and averages, increases or decreases in stock market volume and stock prices, the number of short sales and odd-lot short sales occurring over a given period of time, and the activity and price direction of the most active stocks.

THE FUNDAMENTALS OF STOCKS MADE UNDERSTANDABLE

Ratio Analysis

Critical to making the appropriate stock selections is an understanding of the economic and financial fundamentals of a particular company that may be major factors in driving its stock price. This process begins with an estimate of the company's future revenues and then discerns how this would be affected by certain variables such as the state of the general economy and the extent of competitive market forces that impact on the company in question. Small deviations in these predictions can radically alter any forecast. Basically, however, a company's revenue growth is likely to have a tremendous impact on its quarterly and annual earnings, which should in turn, be reflected in the future price of the company's stock.

There are four measures of common stock performance that all investors should understand. A firm's *earnings per share* are calculated by taking the profit of the company after taxes, subtracting the company's preferred dividends, and dividing this number by the number of common stock shares that are outstanding. The company's *price/earnings ratio,* a measure of how the stock market values a company's stock, is calculated by dividing the market price of a company's stock by the company's earnings per share. Its *dividends per share* figure is found by dividing the company's annual dividends by the number of common stock shares outstanding. Finally, the *dividend yield,* another significant investment measurement, is calculated by dividing a company's annual dividends per share on its stock by the market price per share of the stock.

Dividends have become significant since the enactment of the Tax Reform Act of 1986. Under this legislation, capital gains are taxed at essentially the same rate as dividends. Previously, investors sought capital gains and were willing to hold out longer for them and even perhaps take greater risks because they would be taxed at a much lower rate. Now, however, because both capital gains and dividends are taxed at essentially the same rate, high-dividend-paying stocks and stocks offering steady dividends are seen to be particularly attractive when compared with the volatility of, and possible depression in, the price of a company's stock that may impact the investor's opportunity to secure capital appreciation. This may be altered by future legislation.

All the foregoing measures must be compared with those of similar companies in a given industry, companies of like generic character, and the stock market as a whole, so that individual investors can select stocks that are appropriate for their portfolios.

Industry and Product Life Cycles

When selecting a stock for purchase, it is also important to investigate the life cycle of the industry in which the company operates as well as the life cycles of the company's products so as to select stocks of companies that are likely to register earnings increases and/or provide desired dividend levels. Analysts have discerned four stages in the life cycle of a product or industry that bear significantly on a company's expected earnings. For simplicity, the terms "product" and "industry" are used interchangeably here.

The early stage in the development of an industry, company, or its products is a precarious one for predicting future earnings, because at this stage, it cannot be known if the company will even survive. Nonetheless, it is important to study a company's penetration of its market in terms of its market share and also the projected growth of its customer base. The second stage of development is usually the one of greatest expansion, when the earnings are likely to shoot up to a greater extent than during any of the other stages. After a short period of time, the company enters the third stage, a period of mature growth, where earnings might increase but not to the same extent as they did during the second stage. During the fourth stage, a company's growth stabilizes, slows, or declines. Purchasing stock of a company that has entered this stage has some risk. It may be worthwhile, however, for investors to purchase stock of a company whose growth has stabilized to balance the risks of other stocks held.

Overlying this concept of industry or product life cycle onto the fundamental analytical ones is critical for investors who have relatively good-sized and well-diversified portfolios of stocks. It must be kept in mind, however, that no industry life-cycle or stock fundamental analysis always ensures positive results. Even when market timing is right, industry life-cycle selection is appropriate, and fundamental and technical analyses are correct, the purchase of a particular stock or group of stocks may not yield the positive results expected. For instance, sometimes larger and better capitalized stocks lead a rally, and sometimes the reverse occurs. Sometimes high-price/earnings or low-price/earnings stocks lead rallies. Consequently, it is difficult to identify exactly which stocks are more likely to register the greatest capital appreciation at any time for a given level of risk.

For affluent investors, this problem is particularly significant because they may use fundamental analysis, technical analysis, and industry life cycle and product evaluations to pinpoint the stocks most likely to register the largest capital appreciation during the immediate future, but because there is an obvious need for diversity in risk, their stock purchases end up wide of the expectant mark. They must also balance their portfolios by purchasing stocks in a wide variety of stock categories in appropriate proportions, and also fine-tune their stock selections by industry groups and subgroups. This will be discussed in Chapter 6.

Stock Categories and Groups as Seen by the Affluent Investor

Common stocks can be assigned to certain broad categories, and this, taken together with a sound understanding of the fundamentals of these stocks and the overall financial picture of the companies that issue them, will make the process of stock selection and investment strategy much easier. For investors who purchase stocks in substantial quantities, these categories provide an important way to group stocks available for selection. They also provide a way to structure a portfolio around these groups of stocks that emphasizes the returns that are expected to be provided by any of these categories, as a function of their inherent risks during any stage of the business cycle.

The categories include those with the highest quality and those that appear to be the most speculative. An understanding of these categories is particularly important for the affluent investor.

These investors are most likely to structure a portfolio that is relatively diverse at any particular point in the business cycle in order to have the greatest likelihood of receiving the greatest total return from the portfolio commensurate with their risk posture.

BLUE CHIPS

Blue chip stocks are considered to be stocks of the highest quality and thus, often account for a large proportion of many investors' portfolios. Blue-chip companies' stocks are financially stable and have a history of earnings growth and dividends paid. They are the traditional investment of all investors, particularly the affluent, who have often held these stocks over long periods of time and through all kinds of economic cycles with the result of steadily increasing gains.

Some stocks categorized as blue chip fall from this category while others move into it. Some blue chips have also been vulnerable to credit-quality declines as a result of takeover. Nevertheless, they are generally the more mature companies. Some provide higher dividends than others, while others provide more growth opportunities. Very often, blue chip stocks are relatively costly compared to other stocks particularly during periods of economic uncertainty and market volatility; they hold their value better than other stocks.

GROWTH STOCKS

The traditional stocks that exhibit an above-average potential for price appreciation are growth-oriented ones purchased by a broad universe of investors with varying risk postures. Affluent investors use growth stocks as investment vehicles to capitalize on potential gains in the stock market without great risk; investors with a risk-prone investment posture actually use growth stocks as a risk-leveling tool to balance the greater risks associated with the more speculative stocks in their portfolios.

Although growth-oriented stocks generally provide above-average price appreciation, all other factors being equal, they offer investors little in the way of dividends because most of these monies are poured back into the companies' operations. Growth is fueled by increasing sales and market share that move at rates well above the average for companies in their particular industries. These factors then fuel earnings growth, resulting in the upward movement of the stock's price, which provides the opportunity for investors to reap capital gains.

A key difficulty in identifying stocks that are likely to achieve above-average capital appreciation relates to the fact that growth-oriented companies run the gamut from high quality to questionable in nature. Nevertheless, growth-oriented stocks do provide a greater prospect of an above-average rate of return through capital appreciation than can normally be achieved through stocks that are of very high quality and provide only a moderate amount of capital gains potential or those that do not offer the opportunities for capital gains in large amounts but provide a steady flow of dividend income.

INCOME STOCKS

Income-oriented stocks are among the more traditional equities purchased by affluent investors. These stocks are sometimes bought in large quantities and are used to balance the risk of the more growth-oriented stock portion of an individual's portfolio. They provide good current income as a result of relatively high dividends, but do not offer the opportunities for achieving above-average capital appreciation that come with purchases of growth-oriented stocks. Some income-oriented stocks are high-quality ones, but some are those of large, mature companies.

Income-oriented stocks are sound purchases for affluent investors who are slating a portion of their stock portfolio toward investments that have below average risk potential but offer a substantial amount of current income that increases with the amount of money invested. As a result, affluent investors who invest a large amount of funds in income stocks can also achieve a proportionately larger amount of current income from such investments. Income-oriented stocks may also be used to balance the risk inherent in the purchases of more growth-oriented stocks that depend on market movements and stock price increases for providing capital gains for their investors.

DEFENSIVE STOCKS

For the affluent investor the purchase of defensive stocks at all stages of the business cycle can help to limit the risk of investing in the stock market. Defensive stocks do not decline in price to the same extent as other stocks when the economy trends downward because of consumers' need for these companies' products, which keeps these stocks at a relatively limited price range regardless of the economic climate. Conversely, defensive stocks do not possess the capacity for capital appreciation when the economy moves upward.

Some smaller investors purchase defensive stocks only during periods of economic uncertainty. Later, when the economy seems brighter, these investors sell their defensive stocks and purchase others that have more growth potential. They view the purchases of defensive stocks as investment vehicles that are used during a type of holding period, awaiting an economic correction.

Contrarily, affluent investors who own large amounts of stocks might do well to include defensive stocks in their portfolios at all times but limit purchases during times of economic prosperity and increase purchases during times of economic uncertainty. Defensive stock purchases made during more prosperous times also help to offset any price drops in other stocks in the portfolio. In other words, the diversity of an affluent investor's portfolio, which often requires purchases of a variety of different categories of stocks and a number of stocks within each category, may be helped by defensive stock purchases that moderate the risk inherent in purchases of other stocks.

CYCLICAL STOCKS

As a counterpoint to defensive stocks, cyclical stocks capture growth to a much greater extent than do other stocks as the economy is expanding. They are often viewed as a temporary buying opportunity when investors perceive that it is likely that the economy will grow at a rapid rate sometime in the near future. However, note that when the economy moves downward, these cyclical stocks are generally more prone to price depressions as well.

For the affluent investor who may want to invest a certain percentage of funds in stocks that are more likely to capture capital appreciation when the economy grows, cyclical stocks can be appropriate purchases. They are much more growth oriented than typical growth stocks, but they also carry greater risk. As a result, small investors may only want to invest in cyclical stocks in small amounts during high-growth economic periods. Affluent investors, however, can invest a somewhat larger proportion of their funds in cyclical stocks and may do so when the economy is only beginning to show signs of growth. By the same token, affluent investors who are less risk prone may still want to invest a proportionately greater amount of funds in cyclical stocks, but only when it is obvious that the economy is trending upward. In other words, affluent investors may want to structure a portfolio that is initially weighted toward more conservative stock investments but later restructure the portfolio to take advantage of economic growth with a somewhat substantial proportion of capital allocated for cyclical stock investments.

SPECULATIVE STOCKS

For all practical purposes, speculative stocks offer investors the opportunity to reap the largest gains in rapidly rising markets, but they are also likely to result in the largest losses. For affluent investors, speculative stocks may not be as good investments as other financial instruments. Affluent investors who are more conservative in their investment postures than other investors are likely to shun these types of equities. However, when bought in small or measured quantities during rapidly rising markets, and according to the selection process outlined previously, they can and have helped provide superior returns for investors.

Speculative stocks are expected to provide investors returns based totally on growth; they usually do not pay dividends. Oftentimes, speculative stocks are issued by new companies without track records and only have projections of expected sales growth and resultant earnings on which investors may make decisions. Companies that issue speculative stocks may also offer something new to their investors, for example, a well-established market niche or one that is unusual and that perhaps only the particular company in question can penetrate. They may manufacture a new product that can make a tremendous impact on company finances and earnings, or they may have a management team that can identify the hidden earnings potential of the company and have a plan to achieve it.

Yet most investors, large and small, do not want to engage in idle speculation. The risks are too great. Some investors, however, who have sizable assets to deploy in the stock market and who have a wide-ranging knowledge of a great many stocks (or have investment advisors who have this knowledge) may want to invest a small or modest portion of their funds in speculative stocks during upwardly moving markets. The individual investor most able to do this and who may not feel a severe financial pinch, if the investment turns sour, is the investor with the largest amount of funds on hand. More important, however, is the fact that investors who have developed an in-depth understanding of the market in general and stocks in particular can best take advantage of speculative stocks at the most appropriate moments.

INDUSTRY GROUPS, SUBGROUPS, AND SUPER-SUBGROUPS

To tune the selections of stocks more finely so as to be better able to select the most appropriate ones at any given point in time, all investors, but especially affluent ones, must understand the concept of industry groupings. For instance, at any given point in the business cycle or even within specific stages of it, stocks of certain industry groups and their derivatives provide the investor with greater than average total rates of return than do others.

Years ago, this was not always the case. Industry groups were either in or out of favor throughout an entire business cycle.

In addition, there are a great many subgroups of stocks within these broad industry groupings. There are also narrower breakdowns of stocks that may be called super-subgroups of stocks. It is therefore important for individual investors who are planning to invest substantial funds in the stock market to move their analysis far beyond the broad categories of stocks, such as blue chips and growth stocks. This may be done before the evaluation of a particular stock or a group of stocks by the traditional fundamental and technical analysis methods or after it to add support to the initial analysis.

Much of this evaluation focuses on companies that are about to or are making technological breakthroughs, are developing better management strategies, are hiring or promoting new managers, or are developing a specific market niche or an inordinant increase in market share. These are factors that are more likely to affect particular industry groups, subgroups, or super-subgroups and may provide investors with the chance of greater returns at a given point in the business cycle.

For all practical purposes, there are probably seven major industry groups: capital goods, consumer durables and nondurables, energy, finance, technology, transportation, and utilities. To complicate matters somewhat, each of these industry groups may be categorized under the broad umbrella of one or more of the major stock categories. For example, there are consumer-oriented companies that are cyclical or defensive, and there are energy companies that are cyclical and or more growth oriented. There may also be two types of capital goods companies: one that is cyclical and one that is driven by growth.

Consequently, an analysis of broad industry groups and selecting stocks accordingly is not really the final part of the stock group analytical process. Subgroup and super-subgroup analysis is the next step. For instance, there may be different subgroup transportation companies or combinations of them that may fit under the broad industry group of transportation, for example, airlines and railroads. There are also all types of consumer companies. Consumer subgroup companies may be drug, cosmetic, leisure time, textile and apparel, as well as food and nonfood corporations. Even within the subgroup of food, however, there are a great many super-subgroups, for example, speciality food producers, basic foods producers, and all types of companies that engage in the production of all, some, or a few of these products.

The point of developing at least a basic knowledge of industry groups, subgroups, and super-subgroups is that it helps in the stock selection decisions. It is useful in discerning which stocks may be moving upward in price that are also supported by price increases of their overall industry groups, subgroups, or super-subgroups and are not necessarily increasing in price as a result of their own propulsion. In other words, it is probably better to select a stock in an industry group, subgroup, or super-subgroup if these groups are leading the rally.

For small or average investors who are investing in a few stocks that individuals or analysts have recommended as potentially good purchases or who are buying stocks of rather well-known companies and doing so in small amounts, this type of in-depth industry group analysis may not be all that necessary, and is not likely to be done. For a diversified stock portfolio where holdings are of substantial monetary value, however, it is probably useful to engage in this kind of activity. First, an asset allocation based on broad stock categories groupings such as blue chips, growth, and income stocks should be made, as this forms the foundation of a stock selection process. Then, fundamental and technical analysis together with recommendations from other investment advisors, account managers, or others should point up a group of companies whose stocks are probably good values at that time, are likely to increase in value to the greatest extent in the future, or may provide the best overall return for the risk. These stocks should then be screened for support by the present and expected price increases of their particular industry groups, subgroups, or super-subgroups, or the stocks could be initially isolated by screening these groups. Finally, and perhaps most important, the stocks that are selected should be purchased in the proportion that fits the percentage allocations derived for the individual investor's portfolio by the stock categories that take into account the investor's risk perspective and expectations about the stock market as a whole.

PART 3

Investing in the Bond Market by the Affluent Investor

CHAPTER 7

Bond Basics for the Affluent Investor

For most investors, fixed-income securities or bonds are much more difficult to understand than are stocks. Stock prices can either go up or go down, and an investor can either make money or lose money based on the purchase price of the stock. In addition, many stocks pay quarterly dividends, so the individual investor, on an overall basis, can reap a total rate of return that is composed of the price appreciation of the stock in the market and the dividends paid on a per share basis, all on the amount of money invested. These are comparatively simple concepts, but there is much to investing in bonds.

Bonds provide investors with two ways to earn income: the first is current income or interest earned on the principal amount of money invested, and the second is capital gains if the bond is purchased at a discount or for less than the amount for which it is sold or its face value. Similarly, investors will lose principal if the bond is redeemed (sold) at less than its purchase price, which is reminiscent of how an investor will lose money on a stock that is sold for less than its purchase price. Bond market analysis can get exceedingly more complicated, and much of this will be explained later.

OPPORTUNITIES FOR THE AFFLUENT

Nevertheless, it is critical for all individual investors to understand bond basics, but most especially the affluent, largely because the affluent investor can purchase these securities in large amounts and can purchase a certain amount across a broad spectrum of maturities ranging from 1 year all the way out to 30 years, usually at successively higher interest rate levels. With significant bond market movements the norm and with large investments in bonds made by the affluent, these investors are afforded the possibility of making major structural changes in their portfolios, so as to take advantage of a whole host of market movements and range of relationships in the bond market that result from changes in interest rates or expectations that interest rates will change. Most affluent investors, however, have not taken advantage of these opportunities by developing a bond investment strategy and portfolio management technique. Many also do not totally understand the basics of bond investing beyond what a particular bond will yield on an annual basis in interest income. Therefore, many have greatly limited the range of their fixed-income investments in terms of quality, maturity, and type.

Ironically, some investors may have placed themselves in a higher-risk position than normally desired because they have not been knowledgeable about the bond market. Furthermore, as a function of their risk, many individual investors, particularly the affluent, have sacrificed incremental increases in interest income and capital gains because they have not fully understood the process of investing in fixed-income securities. A lack of understanding inevitably makes investors shy away from this entire field, which, for investors of substantial assets, can be a particularly lucrative one and a field with generally limited relative risk.

At one time, the bond market was a stodgy one without much volatility and in which interest rates did not change appreciably even over such substantial periods of time such as a year or two. Now, however, the bond market can be highly volatile, and this presents substantial problems for those investors who do not have substantial assets to place in fixed-income investments or who, because of that fact, are deeply concerned about their loss of principal. Such investors may have to sell their bonds to take out their principal invested and use it for expenses or to pay for other items. If their bonds drop in price from their original cost, these investors will take a loss. In addition, the investors might not have enough income to offset the loss, because usually a tax loss on bonds may be used to offset certain income.

Conversely, individuals with substantial amounts of money to invest can take some advantage of the volatility of the bond market. More important, they can use their assets to purchase a vast array of bonds covering many credit-quality categories and maturities. They are also capable of waiting out the interest rate cycles and are usually not forced to sell bonds prior to maturity. Furthermore, they are often capable of using the tax loss if bonds are sold at a loss to offset certain income and thus purchase different securities with a greater potential of earning a higher total rate of return.

Small or average investors usually cannot afford to risk purchasing a bond that has a long maturity and worry about whether they may have to sell it before the bond matures at a price below what they paid for it. Many of these investors also do not have enough funds with which to purchase bonds in sequential annual maturities so they have a certain amount of principal coming due every year to reinvest and still receive increasing interest income because of the higher coupon rates on the longer maturities. More important, smaller investors would not have the large amount of interest income coming in to reinvest in other investments. The reinvestment of this interest income can make an enormous impact on the total return of a portfolio.

From a credit-quality standpoint, the affluent are better able to reap greater benefits by receiving higher yields on lesser quality securities. In many cases, the additional yield received for a much smaller amount of principal invested, by the smaller investor, does not necessarily make up for the increased risk borne in investing in lower-credit-quality securities. However, the dollar value of increased interest income provided to those investors who invest a substantial amount of money in lower-rated securities could be significant. Moreover, capital gains may be critically important to increased overall return, especially in volatile interest rate environments, but only if the investor buys discounted securities in large amounts that rise in price. The affluent investor has the funds on hand to make this investment idea a worthwhile one. Additionally, tax-exempt income may be critical to increasing the total return of a portfolio, and this is especially important for affluent investors who may invest a substantial amount of money in municipal bonds whose interest may be exempt from federal, state, and local taxation. Finally, individual investors of substantial size can take great advantage of the differences in yields among different types of securities and various credit-quality ratings as well as yield anomalies within particular sectors of the securities.

In short, affluent investors are perhaps in the best position of all individual investors to increase the total return of their portfolios by developing an investment strategy around a wide range of types of bonds with different maturities and different credit qualities. Affluent investors have the financial resources to take advantage of the myriad opportunities for investing in fixed-income securities and develop investment strategies to maximize the return on their investment but also limit risk. Unfortunately, many affluent investors have not had the time or energy or have developed the understanding to do so and have no real overall investment strategy for the fixed-income portion of their portfolios. They must, however, also know the basics of bonds better than others, and these are not as difficult to understand as many texts in the field would have readers believe.

There are three basic types of fixed-income investments that individual investors purchase in relatively large amounts compared to others: U.S. Treasury securities, corporate bonds, and municipal bonds. A number of publications deal with the factual aspects of these securities, but not much has been written on who should purchase them, when purchase should be made, what amounts should be purchased, and how an individual investor's portfolio should be structured to include all of these securities. It is not necessary to detail all the facts about these kinds of securities, but it is important that investors have a basic understanding of their major characteristics, their advantages and disadvantages for purchase and sale, and some of the more useful investment facts about them.

U.S. GOVERNMENT SECURITIES

U.S. government securities are basically of two types: those issued by the U.S. Treasury and those issued by agencies of the U.S. government. Treasury securities are divided into three types: bonds with maturities longer than 10 years, notes with maturities from 2 years to 10 years, and bills with maturities of less than 1 year, which account for approximately 40 percent of the market in Treasury securities. Bills are issued at a discount and are noninterest bearing. Treasury securities are taxable by the federal government, and not by state and local governments.

Federal agency securities are divided into two groups: those issued by the farm credit system and those issued by mortgage agencies. Mortgage agency securities are taxable by the federal, state, and local governments, while the farm credit system and other types of securities are taxable by the federal government but are tax exempt at the state and local level. Investors should check the taxability of each type of government obligation before purchasing them.

Federal agency securities generally yield more than Treasury securities. At the 2-year maturity level, federal agency securities have yielded approximately 5 to 90 basis points (1 basis point equals 1 one-hundredth of a percentage point) more than Treasuries and at the 10-year maturity level have yielded from about 10 to 140 basis points more than Treasury securities. U.S. government obligations are supposed to be of the highest level of credit quality.

Theoretically, any individual investor can purchase Treasury securities at any maturity, running from 1 year or less in the case of bills to 30 years in the case of bonds. Many who advise affluent investors, however, have noticed that the greatest percentage of their purchases of Treasury securities are of notes having maturities of less than 5 years, often purchasing securities with maturities ranging from the 2 to 5 years. Sometimes they then sell these securities within 6 months or so as bond prices change, making so-called interest rate plays. In other words, these investors may project that interest rates will move down, and they will get increased price appreciation from the securities that they bought. Rather than viewing this investment strategy as a risk-prone one where investors are speculating on changes in interest rates, these investors view the purchase of Treasury securities as relatively safe investments, especially if the purchases and sales are confined to the shorter end of the maturity spectrum.

For individual investors who invest large sums of money, potential price gains can be quite large. If interest rates go up and the price of the individual's Treasury securities falls, the investor can wait until interest rates go down and the price returns to the price at which the securities were purchased or hold them until maturity so they can be redeemed at their face value or par. This affords investors the opportunity of registering a gain if they bought the securities at a discount or at least breaking even if they bought the securities at par. Affluent investors are in a better position to do this than are small investors who could lose principal if interest rates go up and the prices of their securities go down, because they may not be able to wait until the securities mature, as a result of the volatility of the market or the need for the principal invested may force them to sell the securities.

Some securities have minimum denominations for purchase such as $10,000, $25,000, or $50,000, so that they can only be purchased by affluent investors. It should be kept in mind, however, that a number of other U.S. government securities are available for purchase such as savings bonds as well as government obligations of foreign governments, such as those of Canada, the United Kingdom, and those of international development banks.

CORPORATE BONDS

Corporate bonds are taxable debt issued by corporations. Essentially four different types of corporations issue this debt: industrials, utilities, transportation, and finance companies and banks. There are also basically five different types of corporate bonds: first mortgage bonds, debentures, subordinated debentures, convertible bonds, and income bonds.

Traditionally, corporate bonds were purchased by the more affluent investor; small investors were not major purchasers of these types of securities until they were brought to market with a variety of debt-related options that were grafted on to corporate bonds, making them more interesting to such investors. Among the market-related mechanisms that made them more appealing to smaller investors were zero coupons, discounts, and floating- and adjustable-interest-rate features. Today, corporate bonds are purchased in relatively good-sized amounts by individual investors, particularly the affluent.

The credit qualities of corporate bonds are critical factors for investors to consider when purchasing them. Bank and finance corporate securities are divided into two types: those that are asset backed and those that are not. Asset-backed securities include those issued by car company affiliates such as General Motors Acceptance Corporation (GMAC) and Ford Motor Credit. Nonasset-backed corporate securities are generally considered of a lesser credit quality, but not always. Corporate bonds issued by telephone companies are usually rated at the upper end of the credit-quality spectrum. Some bonds of industrial companies used to be the cream of the crop; at one time they were of extremely high credit quality, but over recent years, this perception has changed.

Many companies have been subject to buy-outs with large amounts of debt issued by their acquirers, thus diluting the overall credit quality of the new company. However, some argue further that almost every industrial company is vulnerable to a takeover by another company that uses large amounts of debt to complete the buy-out.

Over the last ten years utility companies have encountered tough financial times. As a group, they have the widest ratings in terms of credit quality. Transportation companies and railroads have issued corporate bonds in large amounts many years ago. Today, they are not a major factor in the marketplace to the extent that other corporate issuers are when taken together.

It is critical for investors to understand the basic credit-quality categories of these types of securities, but it is sufficient to state here that the rating agencies, both Moody's Investors Service and the Standard & Poor's Corporation, assign ratings to most debt securities issued by companies, and these ratings are usually reflective in the way these bonds trade in the marketplace—the higher the rating, the lower the yield. There is also a group of securities called high-yield corporate bonds, so termed because their yields are so far in excess of most other corporate-related debt, largely as a result of the fact that they are either nonrated or carry credit-quality ratings that are below investment grade. These securities will be discussed in the next section. For all investors, but particularly the affluent who may be purchasing these kinds of securities in large amounts, it is perhaps best to rely on the rating agencies as the final arbiter in the assessment of credit quality. It is perhaps also important that the investor have at least some understanding of what goes into these ratings from a financial standpoint.

In today's world, the cash flow of a company is critical to its debt rating. This is so because very often the debt issued to purchase a company may exceed the value of the company's assets. As a result, the credit analysis of corporate bonds has begun to focus on a company's income statement, where it had previously been largely a function of balance sheet analysis. It is even more important to recognize that, for many companies, a volatile stock may even imply a more risky bond of the same company, but this may not necessarily be the case. Bond prices are obviously interest rate sensitive, but so may be a company's success, and this has particular applicability to the high-yield corporate bond market. Analysts also look at a company's earnings power as seen in its competitive position in a particular industry.

In any event, there are certain debt and financial ratios that are important in the analysis of corporate bonds. These include a company's fixed-charge-coverage ratio, its debt in relation to its equity, its liquidity, as well as the protective provisions of its debt, and the ranking of any debt issue in the hierarchy of all its outstanding debt issues. For instance, questions asked about these latter concerns include the following: Are the bonds that an investor is buying the company's most senior securities or are they junior? Are they debentures that are secured or are they junior to a debenture and are not secured? Are they subordinate debentures?

High-Yield Corporate Bonds

Corporate bonds that carry high yields have also been called "junk bonds" by many both in- and outside the investment community. Generally, these securities do not have a rating by the principal rating services or they carry a rating that is below investment grade, as noted earlier. The market itself, therefore, is rather fragmented, with some corporations coming to market with corporate bonds carrying high yields because they are too small to get a rating or for some other reason, while other corporate bonds carry high yields because they have below-investment-grade ratings. Many of these bond issues mature at the 10-year level, so that few of these investments are available for purchase beyond that maturity date.

These bonds have traditionally been purchased by certain types of institutional investors, but over recent years, some affluent individual investors have begun to become involved in the corporate high-yield market. They usually purchase securities in the 5-to 10-year maturity range and are often able to garner especially high yields in relation to other fixed-income securities in the marketplace at that time. These investors do not usually hold these bonds to maturity; it may be more risky to do so, and it may result in forcing them into a more risk-prone posture than what they deem as appropriate. More often than not, these individual investors trade these bonds in the market hoping to capitalize on price appreciation as yields move downward.

MUNICIPAL BONDS

Municipal bonds are generally exempt from federal taxation and are investments that are likely to be especially appealing to the affluent. In some cases, interest earned on purchases of municipal bonds issued in a given state and purchased by a state resident is also exempt from state and local taxes. Formulas can provide an estimate of what a taxable bond would have to earn for an individual in a particular tax bracket to be equivalent, in after-tax yield, to a tax-exempt municipal security. It should also be noted that certain bonds are subject to an individual's alternative minimum tax (AMT), and investors are advised to consult their tax advisors, accountants, and attorneys to see if the interest or a portion of it could be taxable. This is especially critical for affluent investors who may have a large number of tax preference items and therefore may have to pay an AMT. In such a case, a portion of the interest earned on their municipal bonds may be taxable at the federal level. Those bonds subject to the AMT include most classified as private activity municipal bonds issued after August 1, 1986. Essential-purpose bonds, such as many general obligation bonds, are not subject to the AMT. In addition, investors should also take into account, as best as possible, the taxes levied by their states that would ultimately affect the after-tax yield on their municipal securities.

Municipal bonds are basically divided into two types: general obligation and revenue bonds. General obligation bonds are usually secured by the full faith and credit and taxing power of the issuing governmental entity such as a state government, city, town, or school district. Revenue bonds are usually project-oriented securities and are payable from user fees slated for payment of the issuer's debt. Revenue bonds include those issued for public power, housing, transportation, education, water and sewer, and resources recovery and solid waste projects.

CHAPTER 8

Some Bond Investment Strategies

Investing in bonds requires an understanding of the market for fixed-income securities, their yield differences across a spectrum of maturities, and how yields change for different credit ratings and each bond's group category. These concepts will be explained further in this chapter, but it is important to note that they are the foundation for investing in bonds.

BOND INVESTING CONCEPTS MADE COMPREHENDIBLE

Investors usually purchase bonds that have a par or full value of $1000, but the prices of the bonds themselves usually fluctuate in the marketplace from under $1000, say, $900, for a "discount bond," or over $1000, say, $1100 for a "premium bond." Bonds usually pay interest on a semiannual basis, and the principal is usually returned to the investor when the bond matures, a period that can range from 1 year to approximately 30 years. The amount of interest a bond pays is based on its coupon rate, while a bond's current yield is its annual interest income divided by the market price of the bond. The yield to maturity of a bond provides the investor with the total return that can be expected on this investment, including both the coupon income and the capital gain or loss based on the purchase price of the bond or its original discount. Yield to maturity usually assumes that the coupon interest is reinvested at the coupon rate so that it is compounded over time.

It is well known that bond prices fluctuate in the marketplace: when interest rates force bond yields up, prices of bonds in the secondary market go down, and conversely, when interest rates move down forcing yields down, bond prices move up to higher levels. A bond's price at any given time is affected by a variety of factors, including the bond's coupon rate, maturity, credit quality, and call provisions and whether or not and the extent to which, interest income and capital gains are taxable, all as a function of the interest rates in the market.

Some bonds are callable, which means that they can be redeemed by the issuer prior to maturity. Redemption usually occurs when interest rates drop substantially, and the bond issuer can issue similar bonds at a much lower rate. Very often bonds may be redeemed at par, but many bond issues have call protection that do not permit the bond issuer to call the bonds for 10 years. If the issuer decides to call the bonds after that date, the issuer must pay a premium, so that bondholders may be compensated, in part, for the loss of interest income because they may then have to reinvest the principal at lower prevailing rates. An investment strategy that can be used to guard against early bond calls may be to purchase high-yield securities with 10-year call protection or purchase low-coupon deep-discount bonds and hold them to maturity.

The prices of bonds in the market are critical factors in the decision whether to invest. Long-term securities are relatively more price volatile as are low-coupon bonds. Therefore, long-term, low-coupon bonds are more likely to increase or decrease in price when interest rates move in either direction. Similarly, interest rates affect discount bonds to a greater extent than they do bonds selling at or above par. Finally, there is usually not a substantial difference in yield among securities that are issued between the 25- to 30-year maturity level, the longer end of the maturity spectrum.

It should be noted that callable bonds, in many cases, are less volatile pricewise. This is so because as the bonds approach their call date and prices, investors are usually not willing to pay substantially higher prices to purchase these securities because they are likely to lose money if the bonds are called. Investors can take advantage of price volatility in the long end of the market by purchasing securities with longer maturities and receiving higher yield but also trading on the price volatility. Discount bonds tend to be more volatile in price than premium bonds when interest rates change. Consequently, the investor can engage in some speculation as to the direction of interest rates on a quarterly basis and purchase discount bonds accordingly.

Investors may also purchase adjustable-rate securities or so-called floating-rate bonds. This gives the investor price protection in the market if interest rates rise; the investor can usually receive higher rates because the interest rate earned on the bond is adjustable over time. In some instances, these securities are "putable," or may be put by the owner to the issuer at par, so that if interest rates rise and the price drops, the investor will not necessarily lose in price. However, adjustable-rate securities offer the investor fewer opportunities for capital gains and certainly less relative interest income when interest rates are moving down. Investors should check the characteristics of every security they purchase so that they may be certain of the upside and downside potential that can vary widely across all types of bonds, particularly those with adjustable rates.

CREDIT QUALITY IS NOT FREE!

All people like to purchase quality items, and that is especially so for the affluent. It is both a sign of the ability to pay for more expensive items and the desire to do so. Consider the phrase "You get what you pay for." Whatever is purchased will probably last longer, perform better, and even look nicer, but, it costs more to purchase, and individuals must give up some income to make these purchases. This is no more true than in the investment arena, and in the affluent investor's investment thought processes.

Quality measurements can be applied to both stocks and bonds. It is more illusive when used to categorize stocks than it is when employed for the analysis of bonds, however. Quality has a synthetic characteristic when applied to stocks. It implies better companies with greater possibilities for growth and/or providing investors with current income. It may also mean that the stocks of some corporations, for instance, will be outperformed by those of more dazzling high-growth companies. Nevertheless, these are predictions of a human sort and sometimes have a vagueness to them.

Bonds of companies or governments, however, usually carry definable quality imprimaturs. These are products of detailed review, analysis, and evaluation by organizations that have large, expert, and professional staffs whose job it is to make those determinations. Moody's Investors Service and the Standard & Poor's Corporation are two such firms that analyze and provide credit-quality and investment ratings for debt obligations of companies and governments.

Without giving a detailed review of these organizations and their practices, their rankings of long-term debt issues have basically four investment-grade categories. Credit-rating categories that are below investment grade are considered more speculative. The basic categories beginning with the highest credit quality are Aaa, Aa, A, and Baa for Moody's and AAA, AA, A, and BBB for Standard & Poor's. The rating agencies also ascribe subcategories to these groups by using certain symbols. The categories and symbols used for corporate bonds by each service sometimes differ somewhat from those used for municipals. It is sufficient, for the purposes here, to discuss only these symbols, but there are also ratings for short-term notes and other obligations.

To come full circle in the investment arena, an individual purchasing quality pays for it. The higher the investment grade rating on corporate or municipal securities, for instance, the higher the credit quality, and all other things being equal, the lower the relative yield or interest it generally pays.

Nevertheless, there are some market-related anomalies in credit-quality ratings that individual investors, particularly the affluent, can use to their advantage. One is the fact that the principal rating agencies may provide different ratings on a company's or government's debt. As a result, an investor, especially one who is purchasing these securities in large amounts, can take advantage of what may be perceived a lower price for a security that actually might be rated in a higher credit-rating category or a security that may be upgraded. Also, there are securities in a single rating category that may trade much differently from what may be reflected in their ratings. This is particularly true of the triple-A rating category that has no subcategories.

For instance, certain "triple-A"–rated securities trade very cheaply in price relative to others or have much higher yields, sometimes reflective of the yields of "double-A"–rated credits, and others have very low yields, perhaps indicative of their gilt-edged credit quality. Investors can take advantage of these situations and receive greater increased interest income by purchasing higher-yielding securities that are in the same rating category as others. However, it is important to understand that not only are credit-quality ratings reflected in the yields and prices of bonds, but also the market is likely to have wide variances in the prices and resultant yields of bonds within the same rating category.

REVERSE FLIGHT TO QUALITY: AN ALTERNATIVE FOR THE AFFLUENT INVESTOR

As interest rates rise, investors generally seek investments of higher quality, both in the stock and bond market. Very often, this may entail selling securities that are of low to midrange credit quality. However, as interest rates and yield spreads across credit qualities of bonds increase, it may be financially advantageous to purchase securities with slightly lower credit ratings than what the individual investor presently owns. The result to the investor would be sometimes greatly increased yields and interest income, but accompanied by a questionable or unmeasurable amount of increased risk. The affluent may have less concern that these economic problems may affect their investments. At worst, they certainly have the greatest financial ability to weather a potential financial or market storm, and with the larger amount of money they invest on a relative basis, they can garner increased yield and a much greater dollar value of interest income by investing in slightly lower-rated credits when yield spreads are large. Caution should be advised, however, when investors dip into the lowest investment-grade category in buying bonds, especially when interest rates rise greatly.

This process can be accentuated by lengthening the maturity of the bond purchases. For instance, at the 5-year maturity level, the yield difference between a double-A– and a single-A–rated security may be 15 basis points, but at the 20-year maturity, it may be 60 basis points (.60 percent) when interest rates are high as opposed to its usual 40 basis points. In short, increasing yields by lengthening maturities may be dovetailed with lowering the credit quality of bond purchases so that geometrically increasing interest income accrues. This "reverse flight to quality" together with maturity lengthening is not something that average investors normally do, but it is a strategy that can sometimes result in capturing proportionately larger increases in interest income.

Affluent investors can continue this practice into a much later stage of their life cycle because of their ability to maintain a slightly more aggressive posture somewhat longer in light of their substantial asset base and/or income. To be sure, they may not want to, but it does not mean that the opportunity is not there. The smaller investors may do better to evolve into a more conservative investment posture earlier rather than later in life, and also not actively seek to lower the credit quality of their bond investments greatly during this time even if yield spreads are increasing. In addition, the affluent can do this quicker and more aggressively, while it may pay the small or average investor to lower only a certain proportion of the credit quality of the fixed-income portion of their portfolio when yield spreads become large, if at all.

INVESTING IN DIFFERENT TYPES OF BONDS

The basic types of fixed-income securities to be dealt with here are government, corporate, and municipal bonds. The concepts involved have to do with their relative yields, on an after-tax basis, over a spectrum of maturities and credit qualities. The relative shape of the yield curve and yield spread relationships both among sectors of securities such as governments, corporates, and municipals but also within sectors are important considerations in the investment process. (The yield curve is a line that plots the yields of a security at different maturities. Yield spread relationships refer to differences in the yield of the same securities with different credit quality ratings at a given maturity or yield differences of different securities at a given maturity.) These decision-making processes form the basis of developing a bond investment strategy. It is important, however, to take note of the significant market characteristics of government, corporate, and municipal securities as a prelude to developing an investment strategy based on the comparative value of purchasing any of these fixed-income investments for a given individual investor's portfolio, and doing so in varying amounts and proportions over time.

The government securities yield curve can be rising, flat, or inverted, depending on the level and direction of interest rates. This is a significant characteristic of the market for government securities, and it is critical to portfolio decision making. In other words, the yield on government securities may not vary from the shortest maturity to the longest at times, short maturities may also yield considerably less than longer maturities, or in some cases, the short maturities of government securities may yield significantly more, for the same amount of money invested, than the longer maturities. Furthermore, the government securities market is particularly volatile one and responds to a host of economic indicators, both nationwide and worldwide.

Corporate bonds have the same three basic yield curve patterns as government securities. The corporate bond market, however, is less volatile, but it is also less liquid, partly as a result of the sinking fund and term structure of most corporate bonds. The municipal bond yield curve is usually upward sloping, but it may plateau at times. The municipal securities market lags other markets generally so that the yield curve is affected somewhat later. Municipal bonds are usually issued as serials and term issues, meaning that there is a certain amount of principal coming due every year in relatively smaller amounts with a much larger balloon payment sometime later, usually at the 15- to 30-year maturity level.

In making bond purchases, the investor must compare yields in all the bond markets. It is assumed that most fixed-income securities trade off, or are a function of, the slope of the government yield curve and its yield at various maturities. Yet the corporate and municipal bond markets and their respective segments must also be examined to determine what fixed-income securities to purchase and which ones in each market. As noted before, there are basically four types of corporate securities: industrial, utility, transportation, and finance-related securities. Municipal bonds are one of two types: general obligation bonds and revenue bonds.

Any one of these sectors within the corporate or municipal securities market may have triple-A–rated credits, although a few do not. They provide different yields to the investor, even in the "triple-A" or highest-credit-rating grade category. More will be said about these intrasector anomalies later, but it should be sufficient to state that the first step in the bond investment process is to compare the "triple-A" municipal and corporate yield curve to the government yield curve. This is usually done using a composite of each, at any given point in time.

Generally, when comparing these three fixed-income sectors of securities, corporate bonds yield more than governments and government bonds yield more than municipal securities. This is so because corporates are considered to be more risky than governments, but municipal bonds, which are exempt in most cases from federal income taxes and from some state and local income taxes, yield less because on an after-tax basis they should actually yield in a comparable range, among other reasons. The hypothetical relative yield levels are for "triple-A"–rated corporate and municipal bonds are shown in Figure 8-1, together with the government yield curve.

Figure 8-1 shows that the yields of the securities in the sectors involved are all upward sloping and relatively proportionate. However, as noted in **Figure 8-2**, as the government yield curve inverts, the corporate yield curve also does the same, but the municipal yield curve may only flatten. This is when yields on tax-exempt municipal bonds most often, on an after-tax basis for most investors, exceed those of taxable securities, particularly governments, and this usually occurs at the 20-year maturity level or so, when all credit-related and other factors are held constant. Changes in the yield curves could cause yield spreads to widen or contract at any maturity, but may not occur at every maturity. As a result, the investor must look at the maturity spectrum to decide which type of bond is advantageous to purchase and at what maturity.

The next major point in the bond investment decision-making process has to do with an analysis of the generic sectors in both the corporate and municipal market from a yield standpoint. At times, in the corporate area, industrial bonds may yield more

Figure 8-1. Hypothetical Relative Yield Levels for "Triple-A"–Rated Corporate, Government, and Municipal Bonds.

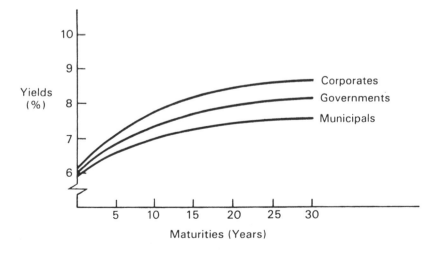

Figure 8-2. Hypothetical Relative Yields when Government Yield Curve Begins to Invert.

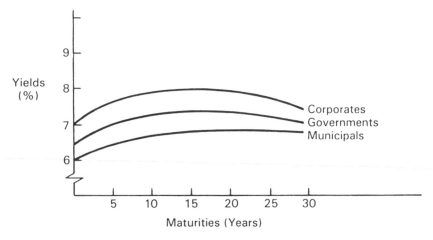

than finance bonds, which may yield more than transportation bonds, which may yield more than utilities, but this may not always be the case for all credit categories and maturities within each sector, and for particular securities within each credit category. In any event, the yield curves for these securities may look like those in Figure 8-3.

Figure 8-3. Hypothetical Relative Yield Levels of Corporate Bonds.

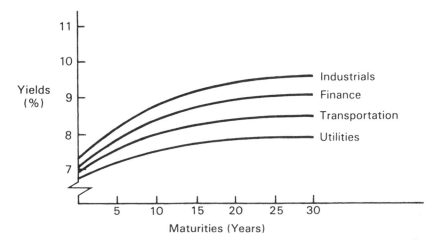

The municipal market may be analyzed in a similar way. General obligation bonds usually yield less than revenue bonds, and certain revenue bonds yield more than others, although this is harder to discern across the board, especially when yields on municipals are partly driven by the supply. In other words, a large supply of a particular type of revenue bond will usually drive up the yields on that type of security, making the prices cheaper in the market and shifting the yield curve vis-à-vis the other revenue bond yield curves.

As noted in Figure 8-4, resource recovery revenue bonds may yield more than hospital bonds, which may yield more than housing bonds, which may yield more than power bonds, which may yield more than transportation bonds, which may yield more than water and sewer bonds, which may yield more than general obligation bonds, as composite yields across all applicable credit-rating categories. Once again it is important to note that this relative yield valuation scale may not necessarily always hold true for all credit rating categories and maturities. For instance, there may be times when hospital bonds may trade either rich or cheap to their historical relationship to housing bonds, and buyers may want to take advantage of that relationship for a time if it is likely to change at some point in the future.

Figure 8-4. Hypothetical Relative Yield Levels of Municipal Bonds.

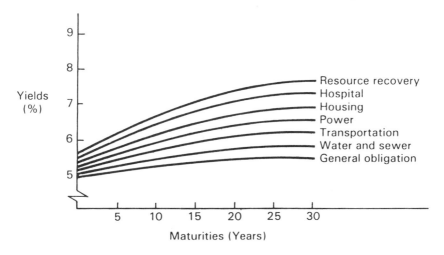

All these yield relationships, as previously discussed, are actually based on the yield relationships of the rating categories themselves and the maturities (see Figure 8-5).

It is obvious that the lower the credit-rating category, the higher the yield, so that Aaa/AAA-rated securities yield less than do Aa/AA-rated securities, which yield less than do A/A-rated security, and which yield less than do Baa/BBB-rated securities. This may be obvious to some, but because of the vagaries of the corporate and municipal bond markets, and because of supply and demand pressures affecting the securities outstanding, an Aa/AA-rated security may yield close to or more than an A/A security at a given maturity in either market, as noted in the following discussion.

Figure 8-5. Yield Relationships of Certain Credit-Rating Categories.

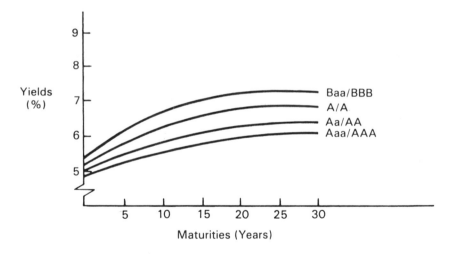

In both the municipal and corporate market, yields can also vacillate across comparable credit-rating categories for different maturities. This is noted in Figure 8-6. This could also happen as the general municipal and corporate yield curves are changing as compared to the government yield curve or as a result of supply and demand pressures in each market.

Figure 8-6. Changing Yield Relationships of Certain Credit-Rating Categories.

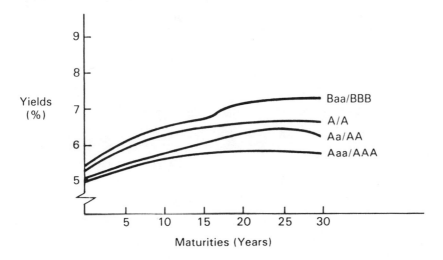

CHAPTER 9

How the Affluent Investor Can Buy Bonds Better

In understanding how to buy bonds, investors should develop an independent investment strategy that takes into account their risk predilections over given stages of the business cycle as well as their expectations about the directions of interest rates and the confidence they have in their predictions. All of this will be reflected in the type and quality of bonds they purchase, in what amounts they purchase them, how much they purchase in a particular maturity range, the amount of funds they put in fixed-income investments that can mature in one year or less, and how the portfolio is altered over time.

For all individual investors, especially those who invest a substantial amount of funds in bonds, fixed-income portfolio strategy essentially begins with a snapshot picture of the Treasury bond yield curve across the entire spectrum of maturities. It also takes into account the differences in yield spreads among government, corporate, and municipal bonds at different maturities in the yield curve. It goes on to compare the amount of interest income from these investments that could be earned on an after-tax basis, thus reducing the taxable and tax-exempt interest income to a common denominator. Then specific securities are selected from the government, corporate, and municipal sectors, based on the relative cheapness or richness (in price) of each type of security within each sector. Ultimately, the process includes accounting for purchases that are discounts or premiums to par value, that are refunded, callable, or noncallable, and the relative price volatility of each. This process, however, should be developed further in ways that accentuate how affluent investors can better take advantage of investing in bonds.

BOND INVESTMENT IDEAS FOR THE AFFLUENT

There are a number of ways in which the affluent investor can gain incrementally increased returns from investing in bonds. The seven listed here do not include every one that is available to investors of means, but they are some major ways in which affluent investors can garner additional returns from the purchase of fixed-income securities.

1. Affluent investors can, in effect, hedge their bets on their expectations of the direction of interest rates by purchasing fixed-income investments in a wider range of maturities. Then, by investing various proportions of funds in each maturity or group of maturities, they can limit the downside risk of investing in a single maturity or group and being wrong in their interest rate expectations. Interest income would continue to accrue and can be reinvested in the more appropriate maturities as interest rates move up or down, and the yield curve changes shape. This will be discussed at greater length later in this chapter.

2. The reinvestment of their unearned income is critical because many affluent investors simply do not live on all this interest income or the principal that comes due. As a result, their portfolio-related activities, including purchases or sales of securi-

ties, vary widely in substance and style from that of smaller investors. As the affluent investors' orientation of the financial environment around them changes, and evaluations are made on a quarterly or intraquarterly basis, the appropriate reinvestment of this unearned income during these periods is an important dimension in changing not necessarily the investor's investment strategy but the general way the portfolio is designed to take advantage of emerging bond market trends.

3. Changes in interest rates cause changes in prices of fixed-income securities, and for the affluent, these price changes can result in wide swings in the dollar value of their bonds, resulting in appreciation or capital gains or in the price depreciation or market-related losses. Capturing these gains and preventing these losses is another significant element in the portfolio strategy for individual investors, but is especially so for investors who have large amounts of funds to invest in all types of fixed-income securities.

4. The sheer number of fixed-income securities available in the marketplace and the sometimes wide price disparities of bonds within specific sectors pose important opportunities for profit taking for affluent investors. Investors can purchase certain bonds or bonds in specific sectors in large amounts and then sell them profitably at a given time period, thus capitalizing on the yield spreads or price disparities in the market. Because of the amount invested by the affluent investor, the dollar amount of capital appreciation received on an annualized basis can assume enormous significance.

5. Affluent investors can also use investment earnings or interest income to invest in sectors of the fixed-income market or purchase securities that are trading "cheap" to the market. The investor can thus take advantage of price disparities in the market without upsetting the existing structure of the portfolio by selling any particular security. This can also be done with any principal that comes due during this period.

6. The affluent investor can also maintain a significant presence in a particular security by holding a maturity in a large amount while depleting some of the holding and using the funds to purchase other securities in order to take advantage of price disparities within or among sectors, all without selling the entire

security. This results in sort of a hedged position that allows the affluent investor the opportunity to continue to hold a significant position in the security, the purchase of which was based on the original expectation of where the market was going, in the hope that expectation might actually turn out to be correct.

7. The affluent investor can also take advantage of widening spreads in high interest rate environments, as noted earlier. Usually when interest rates are high, or as interest rates move upward, there is a widening in yield spreads among credit-quality categories of a single bond sector, and often among sectors themselves. For instance, as interest rates increase, there is a greater difference in yields between higher- and lower-rated bonds as well as proportionately and often substantially higher yields than when interest rates were lower, as previously noted. In most instances, smaller investors become concerned about the economy during high interest rate periods, and there is a so-called flight to quality. Investors begin investing in higher-quality securities because of fear that the economy will impact the earning power of corporations and the financial staying power of governments. In doing this, most investors are sacrificing in-creased yield as yield differentials widen across credit categories and maturities.

DIFFERENT BOND MATURITIES FOR THE AFFLUENT INVESTOR

Generally speaking, most individual investors conceive of three different bond maturity levels beyond 1 year: short, me-dium, and long. (Those that are shorter than 1 year will be discussed later.) Indeed, for most average investors, the shorter end of the maturity spectrum includes those of from 1 up to about 5 years. The intermediate maturity level can range anywhere from 5 years to 15 years. Long maturities may run from 15 to 30 years. Nevertheless, aside from investments of less than 1 year in maturity, there are three basic lengths for the small or average investor, and most individual investors think of investing in fixed-income securities with three basic demarcations in maturi-ties.

Much finer maturity gradations can be employed for managing the fixed-income portion of the affluent investors' portfolio. For the affluent investor, in contrast to the small or average one, there is a general perception of five different maturity levels. This is not to say that investors cannot think in terms of fine-tuning their fixed-income portfolio purchases by investing funds in maturities within these groups. Indeed, the more affluent the investor, the greater the chance of this being done, and the better able the investor is to take advantage of yield differentials across the entire maturity spectrum.

For conceptual purposes and as a basis for investment strategy, however, the five maturity groups for the affluent investor are the shorter-term maturities of 1 to 5 years, the middle-intermediate maturities running from 5 to 10 years, the intermediate maturities of 11 to 15 years, the long-intermediate maturities of 16 to 20 years, and the long maturities of 21 to 30 years. There may even be a sixth maturity, one that could conceivably run from 25 to 30 years, but because not all fixed-income investments go out to the 30-year level, and because yield differentials between 25 and 30 years are usually only modestly different, it may not be worthwhile to think in terms of a two-tiered maturity structure running from 21 to 30 years. However, it may still behoove certain affluent investors to take advantage of differences in yields between those bonds maturing between 21 and 25 years, on the one hand, and those maturing between 26 and 30 years, on the other.

A BASIC MODEL FOR BOND PURCHASES BY THE AFFLUENT

In actively managing a portfolio of fixed-income investments, it is not likely that the investor will hold any purchases until they mature. This is because of changes in the credit quality of the securities, the need of the investor to take a tax loss, changes in the tax laws or residency of a given individual investor, or changes in the technical market positions of the securities. The longer the maturity of any given security in a fixed-income portion of a portfolio, the less likely it will be that the investor will hold that security to maturity. What the individual investor is actually doing is purchasing the best investment at a given point in time, when compared to other available investments in the marketplace. The selling of fixed-income securities and the purchasing of others allows the individual to attempt to gain incremental increases in total return.

Actively managing the fixed-income portion of the portfolio, therefore, inevitably involves moving the maturity schedule of these investments longer or shorter to take advantage of expected changes in interest rates. This may also be aided by investing larger or smaller amounts of money in various fixed-income securities maturing at different points in time. The proportions of funds invested in longer or shorter maturities depend on the investors' degree of confidence in the expectations that interest rates will increase, decrease, or remain the same. For example, if interest rates are expected to move downward and the investor has a great deal of confidence in this projection, then it is much more likely that the investor will invest a greater proportion of funds in securities maturing in the intermediate or long end of the market. If the investor expects interest rates to go down, but the expectation is not made with a great degree of confidence, the investor is likely to place a smaller amount of funds in securities that mature at the intermediate or longer end of the maturity spectrum than he or she would with great confidence.

HOW TO PURCHASE BONDS IN SEQUENTIAL MATURITIES

What all this leads to is purchasing bonds in sequential or staggered maturities where investors invest varying proportions of funds in different maturities at different stages of the interest rate cycle as a result of expectations about the future direction of interest rates that are made with greater or lesser degrees of confidence and based on their given risk posture. This means that investors could put a certain percentage of their assets allocated for fixed-income securities into specific maturities that could range from 1 to 30 years. This concept can be specifically tailored for each investor by purchasing bonds of either higher or lower credit quality and in various amounts at each maturity level. The amount of money used to purchase bonds in any given maturity or all of them taken together can be adjusted for the investor's expectations about the future direction of interest rates. By purchasing bonds of sequential or semisequential (staggered) maturities, investors can, in effect, hedge their expectations about the direction of interest rates and also receive a balanced yield on the total amount of funds invested for a given level of risk.

Without detailing too much of the strategy here, it should be sufficient to note that it is the affluent investor who can best take advantage of purchasing bonds in sequential maturities because of the amount of their investable funds, when compared against the smaller average investor who may only be capable of purchasing a few bonds overall and thus cannot buy a number of bonds in sequential maturities or even reallocate and redeploy funds from one maturity to another maturity as interest rates change or as spreads among sectors of securities, such as corporates, governments, or municipals, or specific securities within these sectors, widen or narrow. This activity is forward looking, and the selections of which maturities to purchase are made based on expectations of interest rate movements together with relative yield spreads at a given point in time for a given level of risk. In general, there are three rules that might be useful.

1. The investor should purchase a greater proportion of bonds with shorter maturities spectrum if yields are expected to move up.

2. The investor should purchase a greater proportion of bonds with longer maturities if yields are expected to drop.

3. As noted, the investor should purchase bonds in various proportions across the entire maturity spectrum if yields are expected to remain the same.

These are very basic rules, and they do not take into account an individual's needs, risk predilections, or the generic types of fixed-income securities such as corporates, governments, or municipal bonds that an investor may want to purchase. They also do not establish any rules or a skeletal investment framework as to which specific maturities or groups of maturities to purchase in larger or smaller proportionate amounts, based on the total funds an affluent investor has to invest in fixed-income securities. Most important, the concepts described here are only the basis of a much more dynamic investment process where funds are reallocated and principal and interest income, both earned and unearned income, is redeployed into bonds with different maturities and credit qualities as interest rates change or yield spreads widen or narrow or are expected to do so.

PART 4

Allocating the Financial Assets of the Affluent Investor

CHAPTER 10

Basic Concepts in Asset Allocation for the Affluent Investor

The investment process for all individual investors, but especially for affluent ones, begins with the allocation of financial assets among the various categories of possible investments. These include stocks, bonds, short-term financial instruments, and cash investments, the breakdowns for which will be discussed later in this chapter. The process varies with the individual's risk perspective, the expected movements of the stock and bond markets, the reallocation of funds and the redeployment of financial assets including earned and unearned income, and the changes in particular of an individual's life cycle. Nevertheless, the appropriate allocation of financial assets in these broad categories is a very first step in the process of investing and, more than any other part of the entire process, does more than most activities to increase or decrease the investors' total return received from their portfolios.

SOME ALLOCATION PRINCIPLES
FOR THE AFFLUENT INVESTOR

For the affluent investor, allocating financial assets into four discrete asset categories causes certain portfolio characteristics to emerge. First, the stock and bond portion of an affluent investor's portfolio is likely to be a much larger segment when compared to the funds placed in cash vehicles or short-term fixed-income instruments with maturities of less than one year (this topic will be discussed further in Chapter 11.) In other words, the total percentage of funds in cash and short-term vehicles is usually smaller than the total percentage invested in stocks and bonds. Second, at any given point in time, any one of the four asset classes of the affluent investor may contain a greater proportion of funds than any of the other three.

Affluent investors are also likely to have a larger proportion of funds invested in stocks through most market conditions than are smaller investors. For instance, if the stock market moves deeply downward, it may be a particular problem for the affluent investor, as noted earlier. Suppose that an affluent investor has a stock financial portfolio of $1 million and loses, in a swift stock market decline, approximately 25 percent of this amount, or $250,000. This is registered as a paper loss, and it is unlikely that the investor would be as hard-pressed financially as would a smaller investor who, during a similar market decline, loses $15,000 out of a total amount of $60,000. The latter investor is much more likely to be distraught, having saved his or her entire life to accrue this amount of funds and having no real ability in the future to make back that $15,000. In addition, the $15,000 loss may greatly impact the small or average investor's life-style and retirement financial picture, whereas the more affluent investor, who still has $750,000 out of $1 million, may decide to ride out the storm and wait until the next bull market to recapture the loss and perhaps even make more money than in the original portfolio of $1 million.

The affluent investor is less likely to liquidate any substantial proportion of financial holdings because this particular loss may not seem like a major problem and indeed may provide other opportunities to purchase stocks that are now undervalued.

Moreover, it is much more likely that the small or average investor will pull back from the stock market or even the financial markets in general. Furthermore, the affluent investor may have additional earned and unearned income coming in so that he or she may experience less emotional upheaval as a result of this loss.

This is not to say that the affluent investor will not be upset over the paper loss. Surely, an individual who loses money in the stock market, regardless of how small or large an investor is, may still register deep concern to a greater or lesser degree. Nevertheless, the actions taken by an affluent investor in the face of these scenarios may be less reactionary than those taken by a small or average investor. This alone is a classic difference between the smaller investors and affluent ones that greatly affects the construction of their financial portfolios, the development of their investment strategies, and their actions as a result of general trends and daily volatility in the financial markets.

POSSIBLE COMBINATIONS OF STOCK AND BOND MARKET MOVEMENTS

First and foremost, there must be a comprehensible method for individual investors, particularly affluent ones, to help them allocate their assets in different market conditions. Surely, no model will encompass all the ways that the stock and bond markets could move, but certain market characteristics that may be isolated to give investors a better understanding of how to allocate their financial assets. Most important, if carried to a logical conclusion, the definable and, to some extent, quantifiable ways in which the markets move and the methods of allocating an individual's financial assets accordingly at least provides a framework for thinking about the investment process. In doing so, this framework may be more finely honed to each investor's individualized case that may include the investor's own expectations about market movements, risk postures, financial needs as a result of his or her life cycle, and overall predisposition about investing in any particular financial vehicle.

In this model, market movements are reduced to their basics. For instance, both the stock and bond markets can, obviously, move up or down or remain stable, meaning prices in each market respectively may increase or decrease. This leads investors to purchase and sell different stocks and bonds in different markets and in larger or smaller amounts to achieve the highest total return on their portfolios while minimizing the risk of loss. These movements could occur either slowly or quickly for either the stock or bond markets or at different rates for each. Furthermore, short-term interest rates or yields on bonds may increase faster than yields on long-term ones or vice versa, or they may not actually move in tandem.

For the purposes of this discussion, however, we will take a more static view of the stock and bond markets. In the models described in this book, the stock and bond markets are slated to move moderately either up or down in price or remain stable for the next one or two quarters, and long- and short-term interest rates are projected to move together proportionately.

There are three possible movements or ways, then, in which the stock and bond market can be expected to perform. These are summarized in Table 10-1. Parts A through C of column I in the table indicate the potential movement of the stock market, and numbers 1 through 3 of column II indicate the potential movement of the bond market.

Table 10-1. Directions of Stock and Bond Market Prices

I	II
A:Stocks up	1:Bonds up
B:Stocks down	2:Bonds down
C:Stocks stable	3:Bonds stable

As shown in Table 10-2, there are nine combinations of market movement possibilities when the two groups of possible movements for the stock and bond markets are combined. Column I of the table shows that the stock market can move up while the bond markets may move up, may move down, or may remain stable. Column II shows that the stock market could move down while the bond markets may move up, may move down, or may remain stable. Finally, column III indicates that while the stock market may remain stable, the bond market may move up, may move down, or may remain stable. This provides the investor with a nine basic cases around which to structure the financial assets of a large portfolio.

Table 10-2. Possible Combinations of Stock
and Bond Market Movements

I	II	III
A:1	B:1	C:1
A:2	B:2	C:2
A:3	B:3	C:3

THE MARKET VOLATILITY AND THE AFFLUENT INVESTOR

A classic problem for individual investors today is their inability to stick with their own investment strategy and asset allocation proportions during periods of stock and bond market volatility. The situation is particularly problematic for investors with smaller financial assets and who may therefore have a deep and overriding concern about risking their capital. This is not to say that some affluent investors may not share a similar concern and, as a result, recoil from investing in financial vehicles that are likely to be more volatile than the average investment. Or, similarly, many affluent investors may pull back from investing in both the stock and the bond markets when either becomes especially volatile. However, with large amounts of capital invested in the stock and bond markets and with the financial wherewithal to ride out much volatility, affluent investors may be more capable of sticking to their own investment strategies when the market abruptly changes course for the short term. As previously noted, investors of smaller size, however, may more quickly retreat when the market turns volatile and liquidate their holdings in particular investments or groups of them that are experiencing greater volatility.

Put differently, the small or average investor appears to have a lower volatility threshold than the affluent investor. To be sure, as noted, some less affluent investors may be able to withstand greater volatility than affluent ones, but on average, this is not likely. From a hypothetical but quantitative standpoint, a stock market decline of 10 percent is likely to force smaller investors from the market to a certain degree, whereas a market decline approximately double that amount or 20 percent may be required to force affluent investors to retreat.

THE APPROPRIATE ASSET MIX

The percentage asset mix has been deemed by most to be the critical determinant in besting the average of any market index on total return basis for any portfolio that includes dividend income, interest income, and capital appreciation on an after-tax basis. This also means besting the market average when the stock market and the bond markets turn downward, or in having fewer losses than normal. It is especially critical for affluent investors, because even a small difference in asset weighting can, when all other factors are controlled for, make a large relative difference in the investment returns because of the size of their portfolios and the income that accrues as a result of that size.

A return of between 1.0 percent and 1.5 percent above the average total rate of return in the market at any given point in time has historically been almost impossible to sustain. One problem is that in any given year, stock prices can go up and down widely; they may achieve an above-average rate of return over the very long haul, but time frames used to measure rates of return are much shorter. As a result, asset allocation among categories of investments is critical. To be sure, moving just 5 percent of a portfolio's assets to or from investments in stocks, bonds, or other financial vehicles could account for a substantial relative difference in the portfolio's total return.

When allocating assets on the basis of percentages, therefore, the investor should avoid extremes. That is, investors should not invest 100 percent of their assets in stocks, bonds, or in any other single category. Such a 100 percent confidence level in a particular category of investment (and no confidence in the others) is an extremely difficult position to justify and to sustain given the history of the markets and the record of stock and bond market predictions by professionals. For instance, if investors invest 100 percent of their assets in stocks, they expect that stock prices will provide a greater rate of return than any other investment, and this implies total confidence in the accuracy of this prediction. The approach to asset mix suggested here is a percentage blend to go with a particular level of confidence and rate of return needed for a given financial situation commensurate with the appropriate level of risk. It is suggested that affluent investors place at most 70 percent of their financial assets in either stocks or bonds, based upon an investor who seeks diversity, while attempting to achieve the highest total return with a limited amount of risk and with certain expectations of future market conditions.

A BASIC ASSET ALLOCATION MODEL FOR THE AFFLUENT INVESTOR

Any model that serves as a framework on which to allocate an individual's financial assets across the four broad categories must have a base case of allocation percentages. All other asset allocation models must take this base case into account as well as the investor's expectations about direction of the financial markets and risk posture. Also this model should be somewhat different for affluent investors as opposed to the smaller or average ones. For the purposes of discussion, the base case is one that expects the stock and bond markets to remain relatively stable. This posture sets the stage for allocating an investor's financial assets. The base case assumes that the investors have an average overall risk posture for both the stock and bond markets. To be sure, asset allocations may differ somewhat from the base case for either group of investors or any particular investor based on their risk posture, their expectations about what will happen in the markets, their life cycle, and their needs for income or cash.

Table 10-3 illustrates a hypothetical base case for asset allocation for the small or average investor, shown in column I of the table, and for the affluent investor, shown in column II.

Table 10-3. Hypothetical Base Case Asset Allocation Models
by Percentage of Funds

	I *Smaller Investors*	II *Affluent Investors*
Stocks	35%	40%
Bonds	35	40
Short-term investments	20	15
Cash	10	5

As can be seen, smaller investors have a greater percentage of assets invested in cash or more liquid instruments and also short-term fixed-income financial vehicles with maturities of less than 1 year. Smaller investors have 10 percent invested in cash and 20 percent in short-term instruments, while affluent investors have 5 percent invested in cash vehicles and 15 percent in short-term instruments. This leaves small or average investors with 70 percent of their funds to be divided between stocks and bonds, but it leaves affluent investors 80 percent of their total financial assets to be used for purchases of stocks and bonds. For the purposes of the base case, investments in stocks and bonds made by both the average and affluent investor are divided evenly.

It is also worth noting that less affluent investors may opt to have a substantially larger proportion of their funds invested in short-term instruments or the more liquid cash financial vehicles, beyond the 20 percent and 10 percent, respectively, than is suggested here. This increase may be a result of either their desire to preserve their financial assets or the need for more liquid investments to pay living expenses or for expensive but needed items. This would reduce the total amount of funds invested in stocks and bonds.

This is not to say that affluent investors may not, at times, have a substantially greater proportion of their financial assets invested in cash and short-term instruments than is depicted in column II of Table 10-3. It does mean, however, that affluent investors are less likely to go this route, largely because of the size of their financial assets, and the fact that 20 percent of their financial assets are invested in cash and short-term investments anyway. Certainly, however, a more conservative investment posture, one that results in a larger proportion of an affluent investor's financial assets being invested in short-term vehicles or cash instruments, can justifiably result during certain stages of the business cycle or when the stock or bond markets are highly volatile. Nevertheless, it would be less likely for the affluent investors to reallocate their financial assets toward greater percentages of investments in short-term and cash instruments than it is for the smaller investors.

Although the issues relating to cash and short-term investments have been briefly discussed here because they relate to the basic asset allocation model, they demand much greater review. Indeed, they bear significantly on the differences in asset allocations made by the affluent and the small or average investor. This topic is covered further in Chapter 11.

Cash and Short-Term Investments for the Affluent Investor

One of the most perplexing if not critical problems facing individual investors today is the question of how much money should be placed in cash instruments as opposed to the amount that should be used to purchase short-term fixed-income investment vehicles during any stage in the investment process or business cycle. Indeed, the concepts involved in this securities selection process relate to the size of the individual investor's portfolio and the investor's risk posture. Often these differentiate affluent investors from small or average ones not only in how the problem is approached but also in what is involved in the selection of cash and short-term investment vehicles for purchase and sale.

THE VIEWS OF DIFFERENT INVESTORS

As noted earlier, short-term investments are typically of the fixed-income variety and can have widely differing yields. They usually come in the form of government bills, notes, or bonds, or even certificates of deposit, all of which can mature anywhere from 30 days to 1 year, thus emphasizing the fixed-income nature of these investment vehicles. Cash instruments, however, are perceived to be investments that are readily liquid such as money market accounts, cash accounts, or savings accounts. Because small or average investors often need to stay relatively liquid to be able to pay for emergencies or even because of their fear that they will lose the principal on their investments, the issue of investing in cash vehicles as opposed to short-term instruments of the fixed-income variety and the extent to which this should or should not be done is one that looms large.

To be sure, small investors perceive that this question has within it an implied deeply demarcated line, emphasizing the ability to get one's hands on one's funds quickly as opposed to waiting for a series of fixed-income investments to mature at a specific but sometimes aggravating rate, even if the maturities are less than 1 year. Small or average investors, therefore, often view the short-term portion of the portfolio as a series of maturities with close to the same yield levels, but that are spaced at some length from one another on the basis of maturity. For smaller investors, the short-term portion of the portfolio means more than simply a place to park available cash.

Because small or average investors may have a need for their funds before the short-term investments come due and they can receive their principal back in whole amounts, these investors view the short-term portion of their portfolio as truly fixed-income maturities and, as a result, tend to shy away from investing sequentially within it. They may do this in two ways. First, they may be more likely to place a larger percentage of their funds in the early maturities of the short-term portion of the portfolio, such as in fixed-income instruments with maturities of 3 or 6 months as opposed to 1 year. Second, smaller investors are more likely to dilute the short-term portion of their portfolio and place proportionately less money in fixed-income instruments with short-term maturities, saving a greater percentage of funds that would be slated for investments of less than 1 year for investing in cash vehicles or more liquid instruments.

THE AFFLUENT INVESTOR'S VIEW

More so than small or average investors, affluent ones are more likely to be able to plan for their episodic needs for capital. They also usually harbor less concern for the overall loss of principal problem in the field of investments. For instance, affluent investors are more capable of planning the purchases of homes of varying sizes and engage in spending habits that usually accompany a more affluent life-style. The closing on houses can be moved up or postponed, mortgages can be refinanced, loans can be secured more readily, and funds can be made available more easily to them on an unsecured basis to cover unanticipated expenditures. In general, affluent investors have a much greater ability to get their hands on funds when needed without liquidating major portions of their portfolio. As a result, the cash portion of an affluent investor's portfolio takes on somewhat less significance if it is kept at the appropriate level to meet some of the investor's unanticipated financial needs.

The short-term fixed-income portion of an affluent investor's portfolio may stand in stark contrast to that of a smaller investor's in size, allocation among maturities, and overall investment strategy. In general, the short-term proportion of an affluent investor's portfolio is also likely to be smaller than that of other investors. In addition, it is more likely to have a greater percentage of its overall funds in fixed-income instruments that mature on the longer end of the short-term portion of a portfolio. This is because these investors may have less of a need for funds at the 3-month or 6-month level, and also and perhaps most important, because it is more likely that they can garner much greater additional income from investing in, say, the 1-year maturity range. This assumes that there are proportionally greater yield advantages from investing in the 1-year maturity range than there are in the 3-month to 6-month maturity range, or that investing at the longer end of the short-term maturity spectrum will yield the investor greater interest income than will investments in the shorter end.

For small or average investors, the need to have cash coming due to meet expenses may far outweigh their need to garner additional interest income. This is especially so when the amount of money invested will actually not yield a substantial dollar amount more in interest to them when they invest in a 1-year fixed-income instrument as opposed to a 3-month or 6-month one. However, for the affluent investor, whose dollar value of funds invested in the short-term portion of the portfolio may be great at times, the ability to garner a much greater dollar amount of interest income by investing proportionately more funds in longer maturity of the short-term portion of the portfolio as opposed to the shorter portion or in cash instruments is a critical dimension to their investment strategy. In other words, while the small or average investor sees the short-term portion of the portfolio as a series of maturities providing additional return but perhaps presenting some investment strategy problems, the affluent investor is more likely to view the short-term portion of the portfolio as a source of substantially higher interest by investing in securities with different or longer short-term maturities.

INVESTING IN NEW SHORTER-TERM SECURITIES

The advent of a variety of market-related debt mechanisms over recent years has created new financial vehicles for investing in cashlike and short-term instruments that are particularly attractive to affluent investors in their quests for increased total rates of return. As noted earlier, there are daily, weekly, and monthly "putable" features of certain securities that allow investors to redeem these securities at par at their respective "put dates," when the investor puts them back to the issuer. There is also often a guaranteed yield provided to the investor. These securities usually yield more than the traditional money market securities that offer a market putlike feature, wherein money can be withdrawn immediately. Put bonds of 7 days' maturity do not require investors to wait long for their funds.

Money market securities, as opposed to savings accounts, can cause investors to lose principal if the bond market drops in price and investors, for some reason, must sell their securities in the market. In addition, some daily put bonds offer investors the opportunity to receive a cash bid, so these securities can also be considered relatively liquid, if their market price is right. These securities carry a two-part credit-quality rating: one for the underlying security and another for the letter of credit or other security feature that backs the put. Daily put securities, as a consequence, are one of the more liquid securities in the market on a relative basis.

It is critical for the affluent investor to understand the opportunities for investment provided by these kinds of securities. For one thing, these securities are most prevalent in the municipal market, where the interest earned is generally tax-exempt. Those individual investors in the highest tax brackets, therefore, can obviously benefit the most from reduced or eliminated taxes on interest earned from income on these securities. Also, and perhaps most important, is the fact that these securities are usually offered only in larger purchasable denominations of $100,000 or more, so that only affluent and institutional investors can take advantage of them. This is not unlike the situations with a number of fixed-income instruments such as the jumbo certificates of deposits that come in denominations of $100,000. Finally, and most significantly, these are appropriate investment vehicles for those who inherit a large sum of money or who have sold stocks or bonds and do not have an immediate plan to invest the available funds, or have a large amount of principal and/or interest coming due at once or within a relatively short period of time and do not know how to deploy it. These situations may require considerations taking a few days at least, and all of them may be endemic to affluent investors.

CASH AND SHORT-TERM ASSET ALLOCATION FOR THE AFFLUENT

For the asset allocation models set forth in this book, it is assumed that there are certain percentages beyond which it is not advisable to invest in a particular stock group or type of bond of a certain maturity or credit quality or stocks and bonds taken as separate groups. This is because there is a risk of having too much confidence in an underlying assumption that prices of stocks or bonds will move in certain directions. The same applies to investments that are used as defensive maneuvers so that putting such a large percentage of one's funds in defensive-type stocks or bonds or even in cash and short-term investments would imply too high a degree of confidence in that defensive position at any given point in time. It could also result in noticeably decreased total rates of return in certain markets, all other things being equal.

For the affluent, the total proportion of funds that perhaps should be invested in cash at any given point in time is about 35 percent, and for short-term investments, the proportion might be limited to about 40 percent. However, it is suggested that at any given time, the total amount invested in both cash and short-term vehicles should not be more than 60 percent so that the investor cannot go to the limits on investing in both cash and short-term instruments, but rather can invest in these vehicles in any proportion up to the 60 percent total limit. Smaller and average investors may require substantially larger proportions of their funds to be invested in cash and short-term investments.

Surely, some individuals may want to put a larger percentage of funds in the cash and/or short-term portions of the portfolio. This cannot be denied, and it may change over time for any investor given his or her particular financial situation, risk posture, and expectations about what is likely to occur in the market. However, while these are rules of thumb, they are nonetheless designed with the affluent investor in mind. The models or cases in this volume, however, do not perceive a need to invest such large percentages of funds in cash or short-term investments.

CHAPTER 12

Asset Allocation for Risk Postures and Market Expectations

Once the percentages of funds that should be invested in each asset category are calculated, they should be adjusted for a variety of investor-related characteristics, thus fine-tuning the allocation in each category to a more individualized dimension. Perhaps the two most important adjustments that must be made have to do with the investor's overall risk posture and the investor's relative expectations that the market will move in the direction that is expected.

ASSET ALLOCATION AND PERCEIVED RISK

When risk was discussed in previous chapters, it was generally defined through the portfolio management process as the purchasing of relatively higher-or lower-risk stocks and bonds. In other words, an individual's risk posture dictates the types of stocks and bonds that he or she purchases or the composition of that portion of the portfolio. This risk posture may be called the investor's "microrisk" perspective. In stocks, risk-averse investors would be more likely to purchase defensive and blue chip stocks. In bonds, risk-averse investors would be more likely to purchase securities of higher credit quality and perhaps even shorter maturities. It was, therefore, expected that individual investors, particularly affluent ones, could simply adjust their portfolios for their own risk predispositions by purchasing either risk-averse investments or those that were somewhat more risky but offered the opportunity of greater gains.

If one were to employ this concept alone to adjust an investment portfolio according to an investor's risk posture, it would be lacking a major component of the risk-related dimension of investment strategy, namely, the individual's general feelings or beliefs about the risk-reward trade-off of investing in broad asset allocation categories such as stocks and bonds, reflected in the relative percentages of funds invested, or the investor's "macrorisk" perspective. For the affluent investor, moreover, this is perhaps the most critical risk-related investment characteristic on which to focus, for the investor to achieve the greatest total return. Although this concept may be difficult to grasp, it may be quantifiable to some extent, and it is critical to allocating financial assets for portfolios of affluent investors.

It is rarely understood how, when, and the extent to which the changes in an individual's financial portfolio occur as a result of their particular macro- and microrisk perceptions. It was generally held, as noted earlier, that any individual investor could alter the risk profile of his or her portfolio by changing the types of investments in either stocks or bonds or both by purchasing or selling securities that are of greater or lesser quality and thus of greater or lesser risk.

At the same time, however, an individual investor may be generally risk averse when it comes to stock purchases or believe that stocks, as a group, pose inordinately greater risks than, for instance, do bonds or other fixed-income securities. This investor, therefore, may have a tendency to purchase fewer stocks as an overall proportion of his or her portfolio than bonds or other financial vehicles that the individual considers less risky regardless of whether or not the investor believes the stock market will move down in price. However, the individual investor may also invest more heavily in risk-averse stocks such as defensive stocks and perhaps also blue chips so that the portfolio is especially risk averse when one considers the fact that the investor has proportionately less funds invested in stocks at the outset.

This construction for the stock portion of an individual's financial portfolio actually stands in stark contrast to one of an individual who has an average proportion of funds invested in stocks at any given time and for any given set of market expectations, indicative of the investor's macrorisk posture, but invests substantially smaller amounts of funds in more risk-averse stocks, reflective of the investor's microrisk perspective. In other words, this investor has more funds devoted to stocks in his or her portfolio than does the former investor, while at the same time, this investor has a smaller relative proportion of funds in the stock part of the portfolio invested in stocks of a somewhat higher than average quality.

The investments of both investors can also be contrasted with those of an individual who has a smaller percentage of funds invested in the stock portion of the portfolio because of an overriding risk-averse posture at the macrorisk level, but still believes that there are some opportunities available in the stock market in particular stocks and, therefore, has an average amount of funds invested in more risk-averse stocks, signifying the investor's microrisk posture.

Obviously, there can be all kinds of permutations and combinations of macro- and microrisk postures of individual investors as seen through their securities purchases. Nevertheless, it is critically important to understand that it is the affluent investor who can best take advantage of market expectations and, as a result of the large amounts of funds available, allocate funds according to the investor's beliefs about the risks inherent in the stock market as a whole, and in particular stocks, when both these risk-related postures become part of the asset allocation and stock purchase process. This differentiation of micro-and macrorisk is very rarely understood and hardly ever taken into account when structuring a portfolio. A further explanation of these concepts will be given in Chapter 13.

THE CONCEPT OF MARKET EXPECTATIONS

Another concept that must be applied to the asset allocation portion of the portfolio management process relates to the relative expectations made by the investor that the markets will move in the directions anticipated or will actually remain relatively stable in the near future. This too lends itself to quantification in some degree, and the concept is particularly useful in structuring an affluent investor's portfolio because purchases and sales of securities in different proportionate amounts must be made on the basis of some probability that a particular market event will occur in the future. Surely, for instance, an investor who steadfastly maintains that the stock market will move up greatly and do so quickly is much more likely to have a portfolio whose assets are allocated quite differently from another who believes that the stock market may move up over time, but is also likely to do so very slowly. These two investors will have different allocation strategies for their portfolios even though they both believe that the stock market will move up and both have similar risk predispositions. (This example takes into account the rate at which the market is expected to move and, as such, is a complex illustration.)

For our purposes of the models described here, it is difficult, if not impossible, to account for all the many expectations that individual investors may have about the markets and all the relative probabilities that these projections will come to pass. Two of them that would be difficult to account for involve the speed at which the markets may move and the extent to which they move within a given period of time. Our models will simply take into account the relative likelihood that the markets will move in the anticipated direction.

PORTFOLIO ADJUSTMENTS FOR MACRORISK POSTURES AND MARKET EXPECTATIONS

The macrorisk postures as they relate to particular asset categories such as stocks or bonds and the relative expectations that an investor may have about what is likely to occur in either the stock or bond markets can be quantified and employed to alter the relative proportions of funds allocated to particular categories of investments.

As a point of departure for this process and for simplicity, the position can be taken that an individual investor may exhibit one of three levels of risk. These are moderately aggressive, average, and moderately conservative (see column I, Table 12-1). As noted previously, they do not encompass all the categories of risk that an investor may have, but, for our discussion, these three categories appear to cover the majority of investors.

Table 12-1. Investor's Risk Postures and Market Expectations

I *Risk Postures*	*II* *Market Expectations*
A:Moderately aggressive	1:Above average
B:Average	2:Average
C:Moderately conservative	3:Below average

Similarly, an individual's expectations about what will happen in the markets may be divided into three categories. These expectations—of an above-average, average, and below-average likelihood that certain events will occur—are listed in column II of Table 12-1. These categories appear to account for the confidence of most investors in any given set of future occurrences, especially those that are three dimensional, such as the possibility that the financial markets will move upward, downward, or stay stable. If one were to quantify these expectations, an above-average expectation that an event will occur, from a probability standpoint, might be 75 percent. An average expectation that an event will occur could be classified on a 50–50 basis. A below-average expectation that an event will occur could be proportioned on the basis that 25 percent of the time the event will occur and 75 percent of the time it will not.

Table 12-2 shows the nine categories that result when the three macrorisk postures are combined with the three categories of probabilities that an expected event could occur some time in the future.

From a conceptual standpoint, these nine categories are not

Table 12-2. Possible Combinations of Risk Postures
and Market Expectations

I	*II*	*III*
A:1	B:1	C:1
A:2	B:2	C:2
A:3	B:3	C:3

unlike the categories shown in Table 10-2 for the direction of movement in stock and bond market prices, when taken together. For instance, an individual can have a moderately aggressive macrorisk posture for the purchases of stocks (or bonds) but have a below-average expectation that the market will move up in the near future. This combination of risk and expectations is shown in column I of Table 12-2, A:3. Similarly, an individual may have moderately conservative macrorisk perspective for purchases of bonds (or stocks), but may have above-average expectations that the market will move up over the near term. This is noted in column III, C:1.

It should be noted, as implied, that an individual's overall risk perspective and expectation about what will occur in a given market should be applied to the stock and bond markets separately, rather than together, for the purposes of asset allocation in the investor's portfolio. To be sure, the investor may have greatly varying risk postures for both the stock and bond markets, and may also harbor different expectations about the likelihood that either will move in an expected direction, and these risk perspectives and expectation probabilities may change over time or within each stage of a business cycle.

To quantify the effect that these two factors may have on the asset allocation proportions of an investor's portfolio, it might be worthwhile to suggest that the percentage of funds allocated to a given asset category be adjusted by 5 percentage points for each relative change from the average in both the investor's risk posture and market expectations. These adjustments should be made to the percentage of funds allocated to a specific asset category. Table 12-3 depicts this.

Column I shows that with an increase in risk posture, from average to moderately aggressive, the investor should place 5

Table 12-3. Percentage of Funds Added or Deducted from Asset
Allocations as a Result of Risk Postures and Market Expectations

I Risk Postures		*II* Market Expectations	
Moderately aggressive	+5%	Above average	+5%
Average	0	Average	0
Moderately conservative	−5	Below average	−5

percentage points more funds than the proportion initially allocated in the particular investment asset category. Similarly, if the investor is moderately conservative, 5 percentage points of the funds initially allocated should be subtracted. The same process should be undertaken when accounting for the relative probability of an individual's expectations that a particular market will move in a defined direction. This is indicated in column II of Table 12-3.

This concept would work as follows. If an investor believes that 40 percent of his or her financial assets should be invested in fixed-income securities based on an initial asset allocation proportion, but the investor is relatively risk averse on a macrolevel for bonds, the individual should probably invest only 35 percent in fixed-income securities. If the investor also expects that it is relatively likely that yields will move up over the short term and consequently has a higher level of expectations, from a probability standpoint, that yields will move up, then the investor should probably deduct another 5 percentage points of the funds allocated purchases of fixed-income securities. This leaves 30 percent of the investor's total funds invested in bonds. This amount can then be adjusted to take into account the investor's microrisk posture as it relates to quality, maturity, and overall risks associated with investing in bonds at that given point in time.

The 5 percent figure is just an approximation to show how this asset allocation process can account for both an investor's risk posture and expectation about what will occur in a market when structuring the investor's financial portfolio. Nevertheless, the use of 5 percentage points as a proportionate addition or deduction from an allocation base case, once it is established, may not be too far off a useful mark. This is so because adding or dropping a total of 10 percentage points to or from the base case creates a difference in total percentages, when applied to any asset category of 20 percent, and this is a substantial difference in the allocation of funds to one category as opposed to one another.

For instance, if 10 percentage points is deducted from the base case percentage allocated toward stocks and another 10 percentage points is added to the amount or proportion of funds invested in bonds, there is an overall difference of 20 percent. For example, if 40 percent of a portfolio's funds are allocated to the stock portion, and this proportion is decreased to 30 percent, while the 40 percent allocated to the bond portion of the portfolio is increased by 10 percentage points to 50 percent, this results in a net difference of 20 percent. To be sure, part of the 10 percent could have been allocated to other asset categories, but this would still accentuate the percentage deduction from the stock category. The application of this concept will be explained in greater detail in Chapter 13.

Asset Allocation Strategies
for Affluent Investors

The following discussions describe how an individual might allocate financial assets for each of the nine cases indicated in Table 10-2 that show how the stock and bond markets may be expected to move. For each case, there is a series of alternative asset allocation apportionments with a description of why each one may be used for a particular investor and when each would be most likely employed. Each case is described with an appropriate title to identify the concept underlying the specific asset allocation alternatives.

PORTFOLIO-RELATED
ASSET ALLOCATION ADJUSTMENTS

The first case also compares the hypothetical asset allocation alternatives for the affluent with one that is likely to be used by the small or average investor. It is probably unnecessary to make this comparison for all the other cases described here. Yet, it is important to provide investors with at least one instance that shows how the assets of a smaller investors might be allocated across the four basic categories of financial investments as opposed to how affluent investors might allocate theirs under similar stock and bond market conditions with the same relative expectations about the market. The base cases are taken from Table 10-3.

Except in the first case, the alternatives in the percentages of funds allocated to each major category of investments do not take into account the investor's microrisk posture. In other words, these alternatives do not discuss the extent to which the investor also changes the composition of securities purchased in each asset category coincident or at variance with the investor's purchases of each major financial asset. For example, even for a given macrorisk posture for stocks as a group, any investor may wish to purchase stocks that carry more or less risk from a microrisk perspective and thus may have a greater chance of achieving higher returns when the stock prices move up or a lesser chance of registering losses when stock prices move down. This particular investor may also want to increase or decrease the relative percentage of funds allocated to the stock market, over time and based on certain market expectations, which is a macrorisk adjustment and also make microrisk adjustments accordingly. These are the classic adjustments that must be made by each individual investor, particularly affluent investors who have substantial amount of funds to invest.

Stated differently, the investor could support the macrorisk asset allocation decisions by restructuring the composition of securities within the bond and stock portions of the portfolio from a microrisk perspective. To the extent that the composition of either portion of the portfolio is altered, it may have an overall effect on the total rate of return for that portion of the portfolio. This relationship may also work in reverse. If the proportion of funds allocated to stocks or bonds is changed as a function of the investor's macrorisk posture, the investor may restructure the composition of either the stock or bond portion of the portfolio or both to take into account the investor's microrisk perspective and focus it toward microrisk perspective that offsets the investor's macrorisk one. For example, an investor who has a more aggressive macrorisk posture as it relates to the stock market may increase the proportion of funds allocated to stocks to a greater than usual extent when the investor expects the stock market to move up, but may change the composition of stock purchases by placing fewer funds in riskier investments and more funds in less risky ones. In any event, these are the types of adjustments that can and should be made when investors allocate funds to different categories of assets. These alternatives will be described only as they relate to the first case, as a result of space limitations.

A Note About Allocation Percentages in the Cases

It should be noted that the percentage allocations in alternative scenarios of certain cases may mirror closely those of others. This may occur because of the limited number of asset allocation alternatives that can be derived from altering the base case by 5 percentage point increments. However, even when some alternative asset allocation percentages are similar but are in two different cases, they were spun off different expectations about what was to occur in the financial markets over the following quarter or two, and/or different macrorisk postures. As a result, the basis for the allocations may be quite different and so may other factors, such as the investor's risk posture, that figured into the proportionate allocations for investment funds.

In addition, the allocation percentages for any single asset in any alternative is not above 70 percent, which is the maximum advisable for an investor who still would like to remain relatively diversified while seeking the highest total return with the smallest amount of risk and with certain expectations of future market conditions. Similarly, other investors may be more conservative in risk profile and, as a result, may wish to allocate a greater proportion of funds to cash and/or short-term investments than is suggested in the following hypothetical cases. The maximum proportion advisable has not been reached in these cases. To be sure, investors may wish to take a more aggressive or more defensive posture toward asset allocation and, therefore, will allocate funds in different proportions than the way in which they are allocated in the cases presented here. Nevertheless, the asset allocation alternatives in these cases are fairly representative of the proportionate way funds may be invested by affluent investors.

CASE 1: CAPITALIZING ON APPRECIATION

In this situation the stock market is expected to move up in price and the bond market is expected to move down in price and, consequently, move up in yield. As a result, most investors would normally take funds out of their fixed-income investments to avoid price losses and await increases in yields and move funds into the stock market to capitalize on price advances.

Table 13-1 shows how this activity is likely to result in changes in asset allocation percentages for both the smaller investor and the affluent one. The small or average investor increases the percentage of funds invested in stocks by 10 percentage points, from 35 percent to 45 percent, and decreases the proportion of funds invested in bonds by 10 percentage points, from 35 percent to 25 percent, as shown. A similar reallocation procedure is undertaken by the affluent investor, in this case, increasing the stock portion of the portfolio from 40 percent to 50 percent and decreasing the amount of funds invested in the bonds from 40 percent to 30 percent. Both investors, in this instance, leave the same proportions of funds in short-term and cash investments.

Table 13-1. Comparison of Investors:
Percentage of Funds Allocated to Assets

	Stocks	*Bonds*	*Short-Term Investments*	*Cash*
Smaller investor				
Base case	35%	35%	20%	10%
Action taken	45	25	20	10
Affluent investor				
Base case	40	40	15	5
Action taken	50	30	15	5

Case 1 is also the only case in this chapter that will have its alternative asset allocation strategies described by showing how an individual investor's expectations of what will occur in the stock and bond markets interact with the investor's macrorisk posture toward either stocks or bonds as well as the investor's microrisk posture toward each of these asset categories and how each may be altered to take the perspective into account. As noted, this case reflects a situation in which the stock market is expected to rise and yields on bonds are also expected to increase, as a result of decreasing bond prices.

The investor, therefore, would purchase stocks in larger proportions and reduce his or her commitment to bonds. If the investor had a more aggressive microrisk posture for stocks and bonds, he or she might buy more growth-oriented stocks, and also limit bond risk by shortening the maturities on the lower percentage of bonds purchased. Additionally, the investor may have a different macrorisk perspective for stocks than for bonds. If the investor has a more aggressive macrorisk posture for stocks, he or she would normally increase the percentage of stocks owned generally, but especially in a market that is expected to have stock prices increase. The opposite would hold if the investor's macrorisk posture was averse to the stock market. The same could apply to the investor's risk posture on a macro basis toward fixed-income securities or bonds.

Table 13-2 shows three other alternative asset allocation strategies for the affluent investor under Case 1.

Table 13-2. Alternative Strategies:
Case 1: Percentage of Funds Allocated to Assets

	Stocks	Bonds	Short-Term Investments	Cash
Base case	40%	40%	15%	5%
Alternative 1	45	35	15	5
Alternative 2	55	25	10	10
Alternative 3	70	15	5	10

Alternative 1 shows that small adjustments are made in the stock and bond portions of the portfolio partly to take into account the expected movements in these markets. The stock portion of the portfolio is increased by 5 percentage points to 45 percent, and the bond portion of the portfolio is decreased by 5 percentage points to 35 percent from its original 40 percent. Furthermore, the percentage of funds allocated to the short-term and cash portions of the portfolio remains the same at 15 percent and 5 percent, respectively.

On an overall basis, the asset allocation changes made under alternative 1 could simply indicate the investor's relatively low expectations that the stock market will move up in price and bonds will drop in price resulting in higher yields, but this may not necessarily be the case. For instance, the individual investor could have a moderately conservative macrorisk posture toward the stock market. Or the investor could have an average risk posture on a macro basis toward the stock portion of the portfolio but could have invested to a much greater extent than would otherwise be the case in more growth-oriented stocks because the investor's microrisk posture toward specific stocks may be of the more aggressive variety. These stocks could be able to capture capital appreciation better in the market so that it is not necessary for the investor to invest a much larger percentage of funds in stocks.

The investor may also harbor a relatively aggressive macro-posture toward fixed-income securities and may therefore lower the percentage invested in bonds by only 5 points. However, the investor's microrisk position may have resulted in the purchasing of securities that are much shorter in maturity so that, as a result of this more conservative microrisk posture, the investor may have shortened considerably the maturities of the bonds to avoid price depression if yields went higher and perhaps also purchased securities of somewhat higher quality all without greatly changing the percentage of funds invested in bonds markedly.

The percentage of funds invested in short-term vehicles has also not changed, perhaps as a result of the low expectation by the investor that bond yield will increase, if at all, and there will be no real change in short-term rates. The investor may have, however, reduced the percentage of funds invested in the long end of the short-term investments of less than 1 year as a hedge against the low expectation that yields will move up across the board. The percentage of funds allocated to cash portion of the portfolio did not increase, and this supports the expectation that there may not be large stock and bond market price movements with the need to have cash readily available to redeploy into these two asset categories.

The increase in the percentage of funds invested in stocks and the decrease in the percentage of funds invested in bonds from 40 percent and 40 percent, respectively, in both categories to 55 percent and 25 percent, respectively, in alternative 2, indicates that there might be higher expectations made by the investor that the stock market will move up and the bond market will move down in price resulting in higher yields. This is supported by a decrease, from 15 percent to 10 percent, in the amount of funds in the short-term portion of the portfolio and an increase from 5 percent to 10 percent in the proportion of funds in cash vehicles under alternative 2.

In addition, it seems that the macrorisk posture toward stocks is more risk prone in alternative 2 as opposed to alternative 1, while the macrorisk posture toward bonds is more conservative. This could be supported, on a microrisk basis, by a larger proportion of funds in growth-oriented stocks under alternative 2 and a larger proportion of funds in somewhat shorter maturities in the bond portion of the portfolio, or, in fact, the macrorisk postures could be mitigated by the investor purchasing fewer growth-oriented stocks and longer-term bonds.

Alternative 3 indicates that there is likely a higher expectation by the investor that the stock market will increase in value and bond yields will drop as a result of prices increasing. Support for this thesis comes from the fact that the investor now invests 70 percent of his or her funds in the stock market and only 15 percent in the bond market. The short-term portion of the portfolio has only 5 percent of the portfolio's overall funds, showing that it is likely that this portion of the portfolio will be affected by changes in interest rates as they move up. The 10 percent of the portfolio that is invested in cash indicates that the investor may need to redeploy these monies into other investments if the stock or bond markets move as expected.

This investor is also likely to have a more macrorisk-prone or aggressive posture toward the stock market and a much more conservative one for the bond market because of the relative proportions of funds invested in each, as noted earlier. Nevertheless, the investor's macrorisk perspective for both stocks and bonds could be supported or mitigated by the composition of the stock and bond portfolio from a micro perspective. The investor could invest more heavily in growth-oriented stocks than would ordinarily be the case or could increase the proportion of funds invested in more defensive stocks.

The same types of strategies could be brought to bear on the bond portion of the portfolio. In this instance, the investor could invest in bonds with shorter maturities or in higher-quality securities, so that the investor's microrisk perspective would be relatively risk averse, and it would support the more conservative macrorisk posture that the investor has toward the bond market. However, the investor may not have shortened the maturities of any large proportion of bonds in the portfolio because the investor has a more risk-prone or moderately aggressive microrisk posture toward the composition of the bond portion of the portfolio even though the investor believes that yields are likely to rise and has a conservative macrorisk posture toward bonds in general.

CASE 2: GOING WITH THE DOUBLE FLOW

In case 2, stock prices are expected to move upward while bond prices are expected to move up and yields will move down. The goal, in the case, would be twofold: to try to capitalize on stock prices increases, while attempting to lock in higher bond yields. Table 13-3 suggests three alternative asset allocation models for the affluent investor using, as their foundation, the base case.

Table 13-3. Case 2: Percentage of Funds
Allocated to Assets

	Stocks	Bonds	Short-Term Investments	Cash
Base case	40%	40%	15%	5%
Alternative 1	45	40	10	5
Alternative 2	40	45	10	5
Alternative 3	50	40	5	5

The most basic rearrangement of the allocation of an investor's assets is suggested by alternative 1, where the proportion of funds allocated to stocks is increased by 5 percentage points from 40 percent to 45 percent, while the proportion of monies placed in short-term securities is decreased by 5 percentage points. This might be indicative of the adjustments made by an individual investor of some means who has an average macrorisk posture for both stocks and bonds and average expectations that the markets will move in the indicated fashion, but would like to capture greater appreciation.

Alternative 2, however, suggests a similar strategy for bonds along the lines suggested in alternative 1 for stocks. In this case, the proportions of funds allocated to the bond portion of the portfolio is increased from 40 percent to 45 percent in an apparent effort to lock in high yields, while the percentage of funds in the short-term portion of the portfolio is again decreased from 15 percent to 10 percent.

Alternative 3 suggests that the investor wants to capture capital appreciation afforded by the stock market to a great extent and is less concerned about locking in yields on bonds and perhaps also believes that the stock market is likely to move to a greater relative degree than the bond market. Consequently, the investor increases the percentage of funds invested in stocks to 50 percent and decreases the percentage of funds allocated to short-term instruments from 15 percent to 5 percent.

CASE 3: CAPTURING APPRECIATION IN A RATE STABLE ENVIRONMENT

The expected movement of the stock market, in this case, is upward, while the bond market is expected to remain stable. The accent here is to capture increases in stock prices. Table 13-4 shows three alternatives that capitalize on increases in stock prices by reallocating funds from the short-term portion of the portfolio to the stock portion or from the bond portion to the stock portion or both.

Table 13-4. Case 3: Percentage of Funds Allocated to Assets

	Stocks	*Bonds*	*Short-Term Investments*	*Cash*
Base case	40%	40%	15%	5%
Alternative 1	50	35	10	5
Alternative 2	55	35	5	5
Alternative 3	60	30	5	5

Alternative 1 shows an increase in the percentage of funds invested in stocks to 50 percent from the original 40 percent committed. The addition comes from a decrease in the proportion of funds invested in bonds and short-term investments from 40 percent to 35 percent and from 15 percent to 10 percent, respectively. Alternative 2 shows a decrease in the proportion of funds invested in short-term vehicles from 15 percent to 5 percent and in bonds from 40 percent to 35 percent and an allocation of this amount to the proportion of funds invested in stocks, increasing the percentage to 55 percent.

Alternative 3 also increases the overall percentage of funds invested in the stock market, this time to 60 percent. The additional funds in this instance come from a reduction of the percentage of monies invested in the bonds and in short-term instruments. The proportion of funds invested in the bond market decreases from 40 percent to 30 percent, and the proportion invested in short-term instruments decreases from 15 percent to 5 percent. In this case, the greater percentage of funds allocated to the stock market indicates a greater interest by the affluent investor in receiving capital appreciation, which reflects the expectation by the investor that the market will move up or that the investor has a more aggressive risk posture toward the stock market.

CASE 4: MAXIMIZING BOND RETURNS

In this case, the stock market is expected to go down while bond prices are expected to move up, so that bond yields over time will move down. The object of an investor's investment strategy, therefore, is to prevent price losses on some stocks while attempting to lock in higher yields on bonds before yields move down and prices become higher than they are at present.

Table 13-5 lists three alternatives for proportioning financial assets across the four basic asset categories. The emphasis in all three alternatives is to decrease the proportion of funds invested in stocks while increasing the proportion of monies used to purchase bonds.

Table 13-5. Case 5: Percentage of Funds
Allocated to Assets

	Stocks	*Bonds*	*Short-Term Investments*	*Cash*
Base case	40%	40%	15%	5%
Alternative 1	30	50	15	5
Alternative 2	15	70	10	5
Alternative 3	20	50	20	10

Alternative 1 shows a decrease from 40 percent to 30 percent of the amount of funds invested in the stock market with a like increase in the amount of funds invested in bonds, rising from 40 percent to 50 percent. There is no change in the percentages of funds invested in cash and short-term instruments, perhaps because the individual does not believe that prices will rise substantially in the short-term fixed-income sector of the market or that a greater relative value can be achieved by investing in longer-term fixed-income securities for increased total return as opposed to keeping the same amount of funds in short-term vehicles.

Alternative 2 suggests that the investor believes the stock market will move downward to a greater extent than does the investor under the other two scenarios. Alternative 2 shows that the investor decreases the proportion of funds invested in stocks from 40 percent to 15 percent, while decreasing the proportion of monies invested in short-term fixed-income instruments from 15 percent to 10 percent and increasing the proportion of funds allocated to bonds from 40 percent to 70 percent. This suggests a greater desire to capture higher bond yields, a greater confidence in bond market expectations, or a more aggressive macro-risk posture. The proportion of funds in cash investments remain the same at 5 percent.

Alternative 3 suggests that the investor is also more concerned about the downward pressure on stock prices. Consequently, the investor decreases the proportion of funds invested in the stock market from 40 percent to 20 percent. It seems, however, that the investor does not necessarily believe that yields will move down quickly and so is not anxious to place a substantially greater proportion of funds in fixed-income securities. As a result, the percentage of funds invested in fixed-income securities under alternative 3 is increased from 40 percent to 50 percent.

The investor, under this alternative, may also have a substantial need for cash over the short term, and this is reflected in an increase in the proportion of funds invested in cash vehicles that increases from 5 percent to 10 percent. This increase may also indicate that the investor wants to keep a larger percentage of funds in cash to take advantage of future movements in either the stock or bond markets when they occur. The increase in the percentage of funds invested in short-term vehicles, that moved from 15 percent to 20 percent, may be indicative of the investor's expectation that yields on short-term securities with maturities of less than one year will also drop in the near future so that locking in greater yields in short-term vehicles would be an appropriate strategy.

CASE 5: BYPASSING MARKET-RELATED PROBLEMS

Case 5 is based on projections that the stock market is likely to move down while bond prices are also expected to drop, and as a result, yields on bonds will move upward. These circumstances suggest that the investor should decrease the amount of funds invested in the stock market and also decrease the proportion of funds invested in bonds as prices drop in order to have the opportunity to lock in higher yields with newer bond purchases when yield levels trend upward again.

Table 13-6 provides three alternative asset allocation strategies that support these suggestions. In these cases, funds are taken from the stock and bond portions of the portfolio and are invested in the cash or short-term categories.

Table 13-6.   Case 5: Percentage of Funds Allocated to Assets

	Stocks	*Bonds*	*Short-Term Investments*	*Cash*
Base case	40%	40%	15%	5%
Alternative 1	30	30	20	20
Alternative 2	25	25	15	35
Alternative 3	25	20	25	30

Alternative 1 is slightly more risk prone from a macro standpoint for both stocks and bonds than is alternative 2. Alternative 1 shows that the proportion of funds invested in both stocks and bonds is decreased from 40 percent to 30 percent for each category, while alternative 2 decreases the proportion of funds invested in these two asset groups an additional 5 percentage points each, dropping the percentages, therefore, to 25 percent for each category.

The main distinction between alternatives 1 and 2 is the proportion of funds allocated to the cash and short-term portions of the portfolio. In alternative 1, the cash and short-term portions of the portfolio are increased from 5 percent and 20 percent to 15 percent and 20 percent, respectively. This may indicate that the investor expects short-term yields to stay at roughly the same level over the near future. Or in another sense, increasing the proportion of funds in short-term fixed-income securities can be sort of a hedge against the possibility that bond yields will not move up to the extent that some expect and, therefore, shows that the investor has a lower expectation that prices on fixed-income securities will drop and, therefore, yields will move up.

This is not the case for the investor under alternative 2. In this situation, the investor believes with greater certainty that stock and bond prices will move downward and, there is a desire to move funds to cash or more liquid instruments. The percentage invested in cash instruments jumps markedly from 5 percent to 35 percent, while the percentage invested in short-term fixed-income securities remains relatively stable perhaps like that under the base case. Alternative 3 is similar to alternative 2, but shows that there is greater confidence in the expected decrease in bond prices or increase in bond yields, or perhaps a lower macrorisk posture toward investing in bonds. As a result, the investor has only 20 percent of his or her funds in bonds. Also 25 percent of the investor's funds are in short-term investments and 30 percent is in cash.

CASE 6: AVOIDING THE BEAR STOCK TREND

In this situation, the stock market is also expected to move downward, but bond prices are expected to remain stable resulting in no real changes in yield. Table 13-7 indicates three alternative asset allocation strategies that can be pursued based on these expectations.

Table 13-7. Case 6: Percentage of Funds
Allocated to Assets

	Stocks	Bonds	Short-Term Investments	Cash
Base case	40%	40%	15%	5%
Alternative 1	25	40	30	5
Alternative 2	20	40	25	15
Alternative 3	30	35	25	10

Alternative 1 is a likely strategy to be pursued. The percentage of funds invested in the stock market is decreased from 40 percent to 25 percent, and these funds are reinvested in short-term vehicles increasing the percentage from 15 percent to 30 percent. The latter change is most likely to occur when an individual believes that yields on short-term fixed-income securities are proportionally greater than the amount of interest that could be garnered from more liquid investments or the investor is not sure that long-term bond prices will remain stable over the near future so that increasing or decreasing the proportion of funds invested in this particular asset category is unnecessary.

Alternative 2 is a slight alteration of the investment strategy pursued under alternative 1. The differences are that the proportion of funds invested in the stock market is now decreased to 20 percent while the proportion of funds invested in cash or more liquid instruments is increased from 5 percent to 15 percent. This indicates that the investor may believe that it may be wise to have additional cash available for any number of reasons. The percentage of funds invested in short-term securities is increased from 15 percent to 25 percent.

Alternative 3 indicates that the investor is either risk averse toward investing in bonds or is not certain that bond prices will remain stable. As a result, the proportion of funds invested in bonds is decreased from 40 percent to 35 percent, while the percentage of funds invested in cash instruments is increased to 10 percent. Still, alternative 3 shows that the investor believes that stock prices will move downward, but perhaps not to the extent that other investors may believe or may not be as risk averse to investing in stocks.

Therefore, the percentage of funds invested in stocks is decreased from 40 percent to 30 percent. Similarly, the short-term fixed-income portion of the portfolio is increased in the amount of funds that are invested in it from 15 percent to 25 percent, indicating that the investor believes it is not likely that short-term yields will increase in the near future as a result of price drops, and additional funds are now available for reallocation and redeployment later.

CASE 7: GOING LONG WHILE WAITING FOR STOCKS

Case 7 suggests that the stock market is likely to remain stable overall, while bond prices may move up forcing yields down. Table 13-8 provides three alternative asset allocation strategies that take advantage of these expected movements.

Table 13-8. Case 7: Percentage
of Funds Allocated to Assets

	Stocks	Bonds	Short-Term Investments	Cash
Base case	40%	40%	15%	5%
Alternative 1	40	45	10	5
Alternative 2	35	55	5	5
Alternative 3	30	60	5	5

Under alternative 1, the percentage of funds allocated to the bond portion of the portfolio is increased from 40 percent to 45 percent to lock in relatively high yields. The additional funds for this asset allocation change are derived from a decrease in the proportion of funds invested in short-term securities. The percentage of funds invested in short-term financial vehicles, therefore, is decreased from 15 percent to 10 percent.

Alternative 2 shows a slightly more active strategy toward the bond portion of the portfolio, which, under this asset allocation model, registers an increase in the percentage of funds invested in it from 40 percent to 55 percent, perhaps also indicating stronger expectations that long-term rates will move down. This decision is supported by the fact that the percentage of funds invested in short-term financial instruments is decreased from 15 percent to 5 percent. Also, the percentage of funds invested in stocks, under this alternative, is decreased from 40 percent to 35 percent, perhaps reflecting that the investor is more risk averse in investing in stocks or does not actually believe that the stock market will remain stable but rather may even move downward somewhat, or that better overall returns can be garnered from fixed-income securities.

Alternative 3 indicates that the percentage of funds invested in bonds is increased from 40 percent to 60 percent, reflecting perhaps greater expectations that bond prices will move up and yields will move down. Alternative 3 also decreases the percentage of funds invested in the stock market from 40 percent to 30 percent and decreases the percentage of funds invested in short-term financial instruments from 15 percent to 5 percent, allocating the remaining funds to investments in bonds, in the expectation of greater returns.

CASE 8: GOING SHORT WHILE WAITING FOR STOCKS

In this situation the stock market is expected to remain stable in overall prices, while the bond market is expected to move down in price, forcing yields up. All three alternatives suggested in Table 13-9 have, as their basic theme, a decrease in the percentage of funds invested in bonds so as to limit price losses and redeploy these monies into other asset categories.

Table 13-9. Case 8: Percentage of Funds
Allocated to Assets

	Stocks	*Bonds*	*Short-Term Investments*	*Cash*
Base case	40%	40%	15%	5%
Alternative 1	40	30	15	15
Alternative 2	45	25	15	15
Alternative 3	50	20	5	25

As one moves from alternative 1 to alternative 3, there is an overall decrease of 5 percentage points in the proportion of funds invested in bonds, after an initial decrease of 10 percentage points in alternative 1 from the base case. Alternative 1 is a likely reaction to the situation in the markets described here. The percentage of funds invested in bonds is decreased from 40 percent to 30 percent, and these funds are redeployed into the cash portion of the portfolio, increasing it by 10 percentage points to 15 percent from its initial 5 percent.

Alternative 2 suggests another decrease of 5 percentage points in the amount of funds allocated to investments in bonds, dropping the total proportion of funds invested from 40 percent to 25 percent. The proportion of funds invested in the more liquid cash instruments is increased from 5 percent to 15 percent, and the proportion of funds invested in stocks is increased from 40 percent to 45 percent.

Alternative 3 shows an asset allocation strategy· that decreases the proportion of funds invested in bonds from 40 percent to 20 percent but increases the proportion of funds invested in stocks from 40 percent to 50 percent, perhaps because the investor believes that the stock market may not remain stable but rather will move up in price somewhat more than the investor under alternative 2 or is more willing to assume risks in the stock markot. Under alternative 3, the percentage of funds invested in short-term financial vehicles is decreased by 10 percentage points from 15 percent to 5 percent, perhaps as the result of the expectation that bond prices as well as prices on short-term financial instruments will decrease and yields will increase. In this instance, the proportion of funds invested in cash instruments is increased markedly from 5 percent to 25 percent partly as a result of the asset allocation strategy pursued for other asset categories, reflecting the investor's expectations that long-and short-term interest rates will move upward.

CASE 9: THE BASE CASE

The parameters of this asset allocation strategy are that the stock and bond markets will remain stable over the near term, and they are at roughly historical averages in both price and yield of markets respectively when both corporate earnings and inflation rates are taken into account. Table 13-10 repeats the base case for the affluent investor shown in Table 13-1 where the asset allocation strategy for the affluent investor differs markedly from that of small or average investors.

Table 13-10. Case 9: Percentage of Funds
Allocated to Assets

	Stocks	*Bonds*	*Short-Term Investments*	*Cash*
Base case	40%	40%	15%	5%

To be sure, some affluent investors may want, for one reason or another, to have a greater proportion of funds invested in cash and short-term instruments in the base case and thus may be forced to liquidate stock or bond holdings or both. In addition, some investors who prefer, in any market environment such as the base case, to have a greater or lesser percentage of funds invested in either stocks or bonds, but it is impossible, for explanatory purposes and in the confines of the space limitations here, to provide and explain every conceivable alternative.

Moreover, the fine-tuning of these basic models, particularly this base case that forms the foundation for the asset allocation strategies in the other eight cases, is one that should be most appropriately left for each individual investor and his or her financial advisors. Nevertheless, none of this can take place absent a total understanding of what the basic market parameters are at a given point in time and what might be considered as some broadly defined possible asset allocation strategies for each particular market environment.

ASSET ALLOCATION ADJUSTMENTS REVISITED

As noted earlier in this chapter, the proportion of funds invested in each asset category for each alternative in the cases can be altered and in some instances radically so, particularly the stock and bond groups. This would come as a result of changes made because of an individual's microrisk posture, namely, that associated with the investor's beliefs about what types of stocks and bonds, and which specific ones, would be the most appropriate investments, given certain expectations about the markets. For the purpose of the models described in this chapter, however, it has been assumed that the proportion of these selected securities has remained at an average overall weighting in terms of risk for all major types of investments within the stock and bond asset groups. Consequently, when the percentage of all funds allocated to stock or bond groups was, hypothetically, increased, the percentage of funds apportioned in each of the major stock categories and bond sectors and maturities was hypothetically increased on a proportionate basis to their original percentage.

What was actually taken into account in the foregoing cases was simply the reallocation and redeployment of funds for an affluent investor with varying macrorisk perspectives for the stock and bond markets and different expectations that the markets would move in the indicated directions. However, the appropriate asset allocation strategy for each individual investor, particularly the affluent investor, must be the result of the subtle interplay of adjustments made for an individual's overall or macrorisk posture for the stock and bond markets and the investor's overall expectations about the directions of the markets, all of which is then fine-tuned by the investor's microrisk perspective as a function of particular stocks and bonds of different stock and bond types. This approach can be employed for each case, but time and space do not permit it here.

CHAPTER 14

Asset Allocation Strategies for Stocks

It is critical for affluent investors, who have sizable assets to invest and who are likely to seek diversity when investing, to have a thorough understanding of how to allocate appropriate proportions of funds to the basic stock categories based on the investors' microrisk postures and expectations of what is likely to occur in the stock market. All this must be taken into account when investors allocate funds to the stock portions of their portfolios. However, these factors are especially important for affluent investors who must develop balanced portfolio approaches for large portfolios so as to reap the greatest total return of funds invested in the stock market commensurate with the limitation of risk in the way that they see as most appropriate.

USING STOCK CATEGORIES AS A BASE

For affluent investors, this concept often entails creating a relatively diversified portfolio of stocks that begins first with the allocation of funds into the broad categories of stocks based on an overall view of each category's relative risk. If the proportion of funds allocated to these broad categories is wrong or inappropriate, it is likely that the greatest total return on the portfolio for the risk involved will not be achieved. This stock investment framework is especially critical for those who invest large sums of money in the stock market because it is used as a base to purchase and sell stocks of specific groups, subgroups, and super-subgroups, and particular stocks.

Indeed, a broadly diversified stock portfolio is more likely to limit the investor's downside risk while optimizing the potential for capital appreciation and total return as a function of that risk during any stage of the business cycle. For instance, at no time will the portfolio be invested in stocks that are so defensive that the investor loses substantial potential gains in growth environments, and at no time will investments in cyclical, speculative, or growth stocks become such a large proportion of the portfolio that the total return on the portfolio, in problematic conditions, would be markedly less than what it could have been.

Furthermore, affluent investors have the assets of sufficient size that can be helpful when they believe that they wish to limit their risk further or when they want to capitalize on potential appreciation. For instance, if they expect the stock market to decline sharply and, as a result, want to restructure their portfolios so as to achieve more risk protection, they have enough assets to reallocate and redeploy to a more defensive posture. Similarly, if affluent investors believe that the stock market is likely to climb steadily and quickly, and it appears to be appropriate to adapt a more aggressive approach, reallocating certain proportions of funds invested in more defensive stock groups and redeploying these funds in more growth-oriented investments can be more easily accomplished.

Much of this can be done by reallocating dividend income or isolating stocks in all categories that have not achieved up the investor's expectations and redeploying these funds. This process is particularly useful in the case of the affluent investor who can operationalize the strategy without altering his or her overall investment approach. The small or average investor, however, may have to which would change the risk posture and investment strategy of a whole portfolio and, in doing so, may really make very little difference in the amount of total return that could be gained or lost because of the small amount of money reallocated and redeployed.

With a working knowledge of the basic categories of stocks, it is possible to devise asset allocation models for the affluent investor according to different risk perspectives and also different expectations about the movement of the stock market.

First, the six broad categories of stocks must be arranged from least risky to most risky on a relative basis—defensive, blue chip, income, growth, cyclical, and speculative—assigning to them numbers 1 through 6, respectively. Stocks in groups 1 through 3 are usually purchased in greater quantities by risk-averse investors, while stocks in groups 4 through 6 are generally purchased by investors in relatively larger quantities when they are more interested in capital appreciation and are somewhat less concerned about the risks involved in investing in these types of stocks.

Surely, all investors can invest in these stocks to a greater or lesser degree, and some will want to invest only in a few categories as opposed to investing in stocks that are representative of all these categories. Other investors may only invest in a few of these categories at any given point in time and, as conditions in the stock market change, may either broaden their investments to include stocks that are in other categories or may even limit their investments to stocks in fewer categories. These options are more the exception than the rule, and this is especially so for affluent investors. They have enough financial assets on hand to purchase stocks in all these categories, and they are also likely to seek a greater diversity in their stock investments in an effort to achieve greater overall return while reducing the risk of investing in either too few stocks of too few categories or overweighting their investments by purchasing stocks of only one or two groups.

STOCK ASSET ALLOCATIONS MODELS
FOR DIFFERENT INVESTORS

As a first step in understanding how any individual investor may divide his or her investable assets into appropriate amounts invested in the six general categories of stocks, it is important to understand what is likely to be the case when the investor invests a prescribed proportion of funds in the various stock categories according to a hypothetical but mathematical and justifiable way. Table 14-1 shows that individual investors may want to diversify holdings in various stock categories while at the same time limiting the risk involved by investing in certain categories in equal proportion to others.

Table 14-1. Percentage of Funds
Allocated to Stock Categories

Stock Categories	I Symmetrical Asset Concept	II Affluent Investors	III Smaller Investors
1	5%	15%	20%
2	15	25	30
3	30	25	25
4	30	20	20
5	15	10	5
6	5	5	0

Column I in the table shows that an individual may want to invest only 5 percent of funds in category 1 or defensive stocks and also only 5 percent in category 6 or speculative stocks. These are considered companion areas because the former is most risk averse and the latter is the most risky. The investor may also want to invest a certain percentage in category 2, namely, blue chip stocks and a similar percentage in category 5, namely, cyclical stocks. These may also be seen as companion categories offering slightly lesser and greater degrees of risk than categories 1 and 6, respectively. Column I indicates that the investor may want to invest 15 percent of the funds allocated to the stock section of the portfolio in each of these categories. Categories 4, income-oriented stocks, and 3, growth stocks, are considered companion categories, too. To reap the highest total return in the portfolio with the minimum amount of risk, the individual investor would want to place the largest share of his or her investable assets in stocks in categories 3 and 4. The proportion of funds remaining is 60 percent, so the investor would place 30 percent in each category.

The point of this analysis is that it seems plausible that the proportion of funds allocated to each of these companion categories should be symmetrical. In other words, 50 percent of the funds are allocated to categories 1 through 3 and 50 percent of the funds are allocated to categories 4 through 6. The greatest proportion of funds, however, is used to purchase income stocks and growth stocks that are both not as riskless or risky in nature as those in other classes of stocks but also are likely to offer the investor the highest total rate of return for the risk when taking capital appreciation and dividend income into account. This symmetrical approach to investing in stock categories certainly is of interest, but it often does not mirror the reality of what an individual should do at any given point in time, and this especially applies to affluent investors.

Column II provides a more realistic interpretation of the percentage of funds that an affluent investor might place in stocks representative of categories 1 through 6. As can be seen, the investor has a greater proportion of funds allocated to the more risk-averse stock categories. For instance, the affluent investor has 15 percent of his or her total funds invested in stocks of the defensive category, 25 percent allocated to blue chip stocks, and another 25 percent used to purchase income-oriented stocks. All three categories that are numbered 1 through 3 are more risk-averse categories, and the total allocated to all three comes to 65 percent, which is substantially more than the 50 percent allocated toward investments in all risk-averse stocks in column I. The remaining 35 percent of monies is placed in stocks of categories 4, 5, and 6 that are growth, cyclical, and speculative stocks, respectively. The amounts allocated to these areas are 20 percent, 10 percent, and 5 percent. This shows that, in a more realistic fashion, individual investors, particularly affluent ones, tend to avoid the more risky categories in favor of less risky ones that are likely to offer some capital gains opportunities as well as provide income.

Column III is representative of the amount of funds that a small or average investor would place, on a percentage basis, in the different stock categories. In categories 1 through 3, the investor places 20 percent, 30 percent, and 25 percent, respectively, and these are the more risk-averse classes of stocks. The total percentage of all three groups comes to 75 percent. The remaining 25 percent of investable funds is placed in stocks of categories 4 and 5, with 20 percent in 4 and 5 percent in 5. No investments are made in speculative stocks.

The allocation depicted in column III shows an emphasis by the investor on conserving principal, perhaps because the investor actually has so little of it. In a broader context, this asset allocation represents a reduced average risk posture, far more risk averse than the risk profile of the affluent investor, although this does not have to be the case. Surely there are small or average investors who may be more risk prone and willing to assume greater risks than affluent or other investors. Nevertheless, a more likely risk posture for the small or average investor is a more conservative one signified by a larger proportion of funds invested in risk-averse stocks with the result that there is less need to reallocate and redeploy these funds among different stock categories as market conditions worsen.

ALLOCATING STOCKS FOR THREE RISK PROFILES OF AFFLUENT INVESTORS

For any investor group, there are different subgroups that represent different risk profiles; this was discussed at length earlier. It is particularly important, however, to identify what might be considered the risk profiles of the affluent investor and provide a hypothetical example for each as to how they would invest funds in each of the six broad categories of stocks.

Column II of Table 14-2 represents the proportionate amount of funds invested in each of the six broad categories of stocks by an affluent investor of an average risk posture. This mirrors column II in Table 14-1.

Table 14-2. Percentage of Funds Allocated
to Stock Categories by Affluent Investors
of Different Risk Profiles

Stock Categories	*I* *Moderately Aggressive*	*II* *Average*	*III* *Moderately Conservative*
1	0%	15%	15%
2	15	25	30
3	30	25	30
4	30	20	20
5	15	10	5
6	10	5	0

The most conservative investor is profiled in column III. This investor has 75 percent of his or her funds in more risk-averse stock investments, namely, 15 percent, 30 percent, and 30 percent in stocks of categories 1, 2, and 3 respectively. The remaining 25 percent of the funds invested in stocks are placed in securities representative of categories 4 and 5, with 20 percent and 5 percent allocated to these groups, respectively. The moderately conservative affluent investor represented by column III allocates funds to the various stock categories in a similar way as the smaller or average investor has done in Table 14-1, column III; both allocating 75 percent to categories 1 through 3 and 25 percent to categories 4 through 6. However, the moderately conservative affluent investor is somewhat less risk averse as can be seen when the proportions of funds allocated to categories 1 through 3 are compared for both types of investors.

Column I in Table 14-2 represents a moderately aggressive affluent investor's allocation of funds to the six stock groups. Normally, one would expect that the allocation of monies by a moderately aggressive investor would be a mirror image of allocations made by a moderately conservative one. In other words, the same proportions of funds allocated to categories 1 through 6 by the moderately conservative investor would be allocated in opposite proportions to categories 6 through 1 by the moderately aggressive one. This may not be so, however.

Indeed, the moderately aggressive affluent investor whose-stock investments are represented by column I of Table 14-2 is still somewhat more conservative than the flip side of the moderately conservative affluent investor. For instance, the total amount of funds allocated to the more risk-prone investments by the moderately aggressive investor totals 55 percent as compared to the 75 percent of monies allocated to the more risk-averse investments by the moderately conservative investor. The remaining 45 percent of the funds allocated to risk-averse stocks by the moderately aggressive investor stands in stark contrast to the 25 percent allocated to the more risky investments by the moderately conservative investor. Consequently, the moderately aggressive investor is not the mirror image or total opposite of the moderately conservative one.

Human nature dictates in this particular hypothetical situation that 75 percent of an investor's funds allocated toward more risky investments would not be an appropriate posture for an investor who is a moderately aggressive affluent one. Yet, the 75 percent figure would, in fact, be the mirror image of the amount invested in the more conservative or risk-averse investments by the moderately conservative investor. In other words, a degree of conservative rationality becomes apparent when an affluent investor adopts a moderately aggressive posture. This also seems to reflect the fact, representative in Table 14-1, that shows it is likely that the average affluent investor will adopt a somewhat more conservative stock asset allocation posture when compared to what might be representative or expected of any average investor who apportions monies slated for the stock investments in a purely mathematical way, one that evenly distributes funds between risk-averse and risk-prone investments.

THE AFFLUENT INVESTOR IN AN UPWARD-MOVING STOCK MARKET

No asset allocation model is static; rather, it must be adapted to changes in the financial markets. Table 14-3 depicts what is likely to occur to the asset allocation strategies of three affluent investors who have different risk perspectives when the stock market is expected to move up from where it is.

Table 14-3. Percentage of Funds Allocated
to Stock Categories by Affluent Investors
of Different Risk Profiles as a Result
of an Expected Stock Market Upturn

Stock Categories	I Moderately Aggressive Stable	Upturn	II Average Stable	Upturn	III Moderately Conservative Stable	Upturn
1	0%	0%	15%	10%	15%	15%
2	15	10	25	20	30	25
3	30	25	25	25	30	25
4	30	35	20	25	20	25
5	15	20	10	15	5	10
6	10	10	5	5	0	0

As indicated in column II, four changes in stock asset allocation occur for an affluent investor with an average risk posture. Changes are made in stock categories 1, 2, 4, and 5. As the stock market moves up, this particular affluent investor seeks to take advantage of the appreciation and thus total return possibilities, while limiting the chance that total return will be mitigated by too heavy a weighting of the funds invested in stocks that are less likely to benefit from market upturns. In other words, the investor moves some funds out of risk-averse investments and into more risk-prone ones as long as the stock market moves upward. Therefore, the percentage of funds allocated to categories 1 and 2 is reduced by 5 percentage points overall each, and the percentage of funds used to purchase stocks representative of categories 4 and 5 is increased by 5 percentage points each.

Column III represents the moderately conservative affluent investor, and this model also shows a movement of funds among stock categories in an upward market that seeks to take advantage of the greater possibility of capital appreciation. The proportion of funds invested in stock categories 4 and 5 is increased by 5 percentage points each. In this case, however, the more conservative investor lowers the percentage of funds in categories 2 and 3, which are the blue chip and income-oriented stock groups, while not decreasing the amount of funds allocated in the defensive stock group, category 1.

The moderately aggressive affluent investor, represented in column I, also increases by 5 percentage points the proportion of funds allocated to stock in categories 4 and 5, but leaves the same 10 percent allocation in category 6, the more speculative stock group, as the result of the tendency of investors to pull back slightly in moving funds to the most risky investments. In addition, the moderately aggressive affluent investor lowers the percentage of funds allocated to the more risk averse categories 2 and 3 by 5 percentage points each.

THE AFFLUENT INVESTOR IN A DOWNWARD-MOVING STOCK MARKET

Table 14-4 shows the stock allocation percentages of three affluent investors of different risk perspectives and how they change when the market is expected to move downward. The affluent investor of an average risk posture depicted in column II increases the proportions of funds allocated to the risk-averse categories and decreases the proportion allocated to the risk-prone ones. Categories 1 through 3 are increased by 5 percentage points, and categories 4 through 6 are decreased by 5 percentage points, a more conservative approach than in a market upturn.

Table 14-4. Percentage of Funds Allocated
to Stock Categories by Affluent Investors
of Different Risk Profiles as a Result
of an Expected Stock Market Downturn

	I Moderately Aggressive			*II* Average		*III* Moderately Conservative	
Stock Categories	*Stable*	*Downturn A*	*B*	*Stable*	*Downturn*	*Stable*	*Downturn*
1	0%	5%	10%	15%	20%	15%	20%
2	15	25	30	25	30	30	35
3	30	30	30	25	30	30	30
4	30	25	25	20	15	20	15
5	15	10	5	10	5	5	0
6	10	5	0	5	0	0	0

Column III, the moderately conservative investor, also reflects a somewhat similar change. The amount of funds allocated to stock categories 4 and 5 is each decreased by 5 percentage points and the amount of funds allocated to categories 1 and 2 is increased by 5 percentage points. In other words, as the stock market moves downward, a greater proportion of funds is allocated to the more risk-averse categories, and a smaller proportion of funds is allocated to the categories that are more risk prone.

A more interesting concept in this hypothetical stock allocation table is exemplified in column I, and this represents the changes in stock allocation made by the moderately aggressive investor as the stock market moves down. As shown here, the moderately aggressive investor may adopt one of two profiles. Profile A is slightly more risky than is profile B. As the stock market moves down, the more aggressive investor would naturally seek to lower the percentage of funds invested in the more risky stock categories, namely, 4, 5, and 6. In profile A, the moderately aggressive affluent investor lowers the proportion of funds invested in each of these categories by approximately 5 percentage points and increases the proportion of funds allocated to more the risk-averse stocks of categories 1 and 2 by 5 percentage points and 10 percentage points, respectively.

In profile B, however, the moderately aggressive investor exhibits a tendency to be somewhat more concerned about the risks involved in having a good amount of funds invested in categories 5 and 6, namely, those stocks that are cyclical and speculative in nature. This investor, therefore, drops the percentage of funds allocated to categories 5 and 6 by 10 percentage points from the original amount as opposed to 5 percentage points under profile A. Similarly, this investor under profile B increases the amount of funds allocated to the more risk-averse stock of categories 1 and 2 by increasing the percentages 10 and 15 percentage points, respectively, as opposed to increasing them only 5 and 10 percentage points as shown in profile A that represents the more risk-prone moderately aggressive investor.

What this shows is that a moderately aggressive investor may be more aggressive on a relative basis when the market moves upward, but when the stock market moves down, may

exhibit a tendency to be more risk averse than would normally be
the case as exempled by increases or decreases in the proportionate amount of funds allocated to different stock classes. It is a
subtle concept indeed, but it does, in fact, take into account the
changes in asset allocations made within general risk classes for
certain expected market conditions. Also, there is more likely to
be a greater deviation within the moderately aggressive class as
the market moves downward than there is in the moderately
conservative one because the proportion of funds invested in the
more risk-averse investments by moderately conservative investors is already large. Where there is a great opportunity to lose
money and when there is a good proportion of funds invested in
the more risky investments, investors, even those with moderately aggressive risk postures, may pull back to greater extent
than would be expected. This actually reduces their risk without
greatly changing their overall risk profile that is represented by
the total proportion of funds allocated to various stock categories.

STOCK ASSET ALLOCATION FOR THE AFFLUENT INVESTOR AT DIFFERENT STAGES OF THE LIFE CYCLE

As discussed previously at some length, the older individual
investors become, the more conservative their investments are
likely to be. This is certainly true for affluent investors, but they
seem to have more leeway, even as they get older, largely because
of the size of their assets. It may be appropriate, therefore, for the
affluent to become only somewhat more conservative in how they
invest in the stock market later in life. This may entail moving
from a moderately aggressive risk posture to an average one or
from an average one to a moderately conservative one. Thus,
affluent investors may reduce their risk postures by one level at
the appropriate times during their lives.

This would change the proportion of funds they allocate to
each of the six classes of stocks at different stages of their lives and
also account for the fact that their investments should be more

conservative. This is not to say that these suggestions based on hypothetical cases should be adopted uniformly or that they apply to every affluent investor. Nevertheless, if appropriately developed with a proper asset allocation strategy, the idea can be then fine-tuned for each affluent investor.

CHAPTER 15

Asset Allocation Strategies for Bonds

Asset allocation strategies for bonds must be based on the proportionate amount of funds used to purchase bonds in various maturities, and adjustments must be made for the expected direction of interest rates. This involves the movement of funds in large amounts, typical of the affluent investor's capabilities, from one bond maturity to another or from one group of maturities to another.

A FOUR-STEP BOND ASSET ALLOCATION PROCESS

The movement of funds, however, cannot be accomplished effectively in one step, and what is more important, it may not be a good idea to undertake such a move until stock is taken of the projected interest rate climate over two or more quarters. As a result, the movement of a certain percentage of funds will be based on expectations about interest rates and, then later, on a comparison of those expectations and their veracity coupled with new expectations, which would lead the investor to move an incrementally increased percentage of funds to investments that mirror the new or confirmed expectation of the direction interest rates. This process is likely to provide greater than average total returns on the portfolio.

Table 15-1 shows the percentage movement of funds in four quarterly stages for bonds with maturities ranging from 1 to 30 years when rates are expected to move down after a period when interest rates were moving up and bond prices were decreasing. As the investor's expectations about the downward trend in interest rates are confirmed at the end of each quarter, the investor moves a greater proportion of funds into the longer maturities so that bonds with higher yields are purchased, and these yields can be locked in as interest rates move 'downward. The opposite scenario can be used when interest rates are expected to move up.

Table 15-1. Four Stages of Asset Allocation
by Bond Maturities in Percentages

| Stages | Maturity Groups (Years) | | | | |
	1–5	*6–10*	*11–15*	*16–20*	*21–30*
1	40%	25%	20%	10%	5%
2	30	20	20	15	15
3	15	15	20	20	30
4	5	10	20	25	40

THE SPEED AND AMOUNT OF FUND MOVEMENTS

The reallocation of funds and redeployment of monies including the sale of some securities and the purchase of others with the newly available funds, can be done at faster or slower paces. For instance, interest rates (the prime rate) generally have ranged between roughly 5 percent and 21 percent over the last 40 years or so, so that interest rates at a midlevel could force investors to move securities at a relatively moderate pace, if interest rates are expected to move up, for instance. If interest rates are hovering at the high end of this continuum and are expected to move downward, investors should reallocate their funds more quickly to different maturities because interest rates could go down a lot farther than if they were at an average or low level. The quicker rates move down and the greater the possible downward movement, the greater the chance for investors to lose the opportunity of locking in higher yields. If, however, interest rates are at the low end of this continuum and they are moving downward, investors could reallocate their funds to longer maturities at a much slower pace because interest rates may not have too far to go, and they might not cause investors to lose that much additional yield in the short term.

Similarly, if interest rates are at the high end of the interest rate continuum, and they are expected to move up, investors will not ultimately lose as much if prices on their securities drop so that they can go somewhat slower in allocating funds to shorter maturities in the hope that once interest rates reach a peak, they can purchase bonds with higher interest rates. If interest rates are at the low end of the interest rate scale and are expected to move up, the rates themselves have substantial room to move up in yield so that prices can go down markedly and yields may move quickly. As a result, investors should allocate funds to the shorter maturities quicker so that they will not lose substantial amounts of money to price drops, and so they can be prepared to invest when rates appear to reach a peak. All of this is not to say that in high interest rate environments yields cannot still move up quickly or move down quickly in low interest rate environments. Rather, it is just a way of estimating the amount of an investor's potential loss within a given time frame.

As interest rates generally move downward for a given period of time from a position of average yield, the objective is for the investor to lock in higher yields by purchasing bonds with longer maturities. For the small investor, the movement to do this is likely to be slower as funds are deployed more cautiously, with less necessity for the investor to capture the highest yield possible at a given point in time and less funds with which to do. A faster purchase paced investor is at somewhat more risk if yields then move up markedly and prices drop, and there is a need to sell these newly purchased longer-term securities. For the affluent investor, the movement to lock in higher yields can be quicker, so the investor can begin to purchase longer maturities, and do so by more heavily weighting the amount of funds invested in longer maturities, in contrast to the investment process of the small investor in this type of situation. The affluent investor may be better prepared to wait out the next cycle.

As the result of the relative amount of funds invested, the affluent investor can have a larger percentage of funds invested in maturities that are beyond the short range than can the small or average investor. As long as interest rates remain at the same levels, the affluent investor can take advantage of garnering extra yield by purchasing a larger proportion of securities with intermediate- or longer-term maturities. This would be especially useful if interest rates move downward, and the investor can lock in higher rates of return having a greater percentage of funds in longer maturities and also by moving a certain proportionate amount of their funds into longer-term maturities.

As interest rates move generally upward for a time from an average yield position, there is also a somewhat different speed with which small or average investors reallocate funds in the bond portions of their portfolios as opposed to how more affluent investors would do so. The small investor would generally be concerned about the continuing drop in price of the present fixed-income securities that they hold as a result of interest rate increases. Consequently, these investors are more likely to move relatively larger proportions of funds that are invested in fixed-income instruments into the intermediate or shorter ranges at quicker paces than would affluent investors. The more affluent investors may want to, and indeed actually can, keep a somewhat larger proportion of their funds in the longer maturities because they are better equipped to weather the interest rate cycle as rates move back down and the prices on their outstanding securities increase or at least move upward back to where they originally were before increasing yields forced their bond prices down.

In the interest rate scenarios set forth here, we are assuming that both shorter- and longer-term rates move together in the same proportionate amounts, that they are not moving in opposite directions, and that they are not moving substantially quicker than each other beyond the normal relative or proportionate movements. Like other models described in this text, this concept is designed to foster the development of a pattern of thinking, although the idea may not always mirror reality.

Indeed, as noted earlier, there are times when shorter-term rates may increase, while long-term rates remain stagnant, thus resulting in a flattening of the yield curve. This is certainly an event of which investors, particularly the affluent, can take advantage. One important reason is that the affluent investor may already have purchased bonds in sequential maturities.

RISK AND MARKET EXPECTATIONS IN BOND PURCHASES

When an affluent investor invests funds in fixed-income securities with different amounts going to purchase securities within different maturity ranges, there should be a reason, relative to an investor's risk posture, for how much is allocated to each maturity or group of maturities. At a very basic level, there are three underlying assumptions that must be made. The first is the relative level of interest rates, the second is the direction of interest rates, and the third is the risk posture of the investor. For the purposes of discussion and as a basis for Tables 15-2 and 15-3, it is assumed that interest rates are approximately average and the yield curve is somewhat upwardly sloping. The second assumption is that yields are expected to decrease or increase with an average level of confidence in the expectation. The third assumption relates to the three risk postures of the affluent investors.

As noted in Table 15-2, when interest rates are expected to drop, investors invest a larger proportion of funds in bonds with longer maturities. However, the moderately aggressive investor places a greater proportionate amount of funds in the longer maturities than does the moderately conservative or the average if the investor expects interest rates to decline.

Table 15-2. Percentage of Funds Allocated by Maturity
for Different Risk-Oriented Affluent Investors
when Interest Rates Are Expected to Drop

	Maturity Groups (Years)				
Risk Orientation	1–5	6–10	11–15	16–20	21–30
Moderately conservative	15%	15%	20%	20%	30%
Average	5	10	20	25	40
Moderately aggressive	0	10	10	30	50

As shown in Table 15-3, if interest rates are expected to move up, the largest share of their funds is invested in the shortest maturities. Moderately aggressive investors seeking higher yields are still likely to have a smaller percentage of their investable funds placed in longer-term maturities as opposed to investors with more risk-averse postures. Moderately conservative and average investors who are more likely to fear that holding securities of longer maturities may result in price declines that the investors are not willing to accept have fewer funds in the longer maturities of the bond portion of the portfolio.

Table 15-3. Percentage of Funds Allocated by Maturity
for Different Risk-Oriented Affluent Investors
when Interest Rates Are Expected to Rise

	Maturity Groups (Years)				
Risk Orientation	1–5	6–10	11–15	16–20	21–30
Moderately conservative	50%	30%	10%	10%	0%
Average	40	25	20	10	5
Moderately aggressive	30	20	20	15	15

BOND SWAPS

Almost every book on fixed-income securities contains a section on bond swaps, that is, the selling of a particular bond or group of bonds and the simultaneous purchasing of another bond or group of bonds that are close to, but not exactly, the same resulting in a different overall effect on the portfolio. This could include the improvement, maintenance, or a decline in credit quality, or change in annual income, face value, maturity, or even the creation of a tax gain or loss.

However, when sales or purchases are made for the bond portion of a portfolio or when purchases are made with the proceeds from the sales, the transactions do not necessarily have to take the form of bond swaps. Rather, the transactions may simply represent the sale of securities and the purchase of others perhaps in anticipation of interest rate movements, to achieve a better rate of return over the long term, or for any other reason. While there may be a general improvement of credit quality of the bond portion of the portfolio, or the maturity structure may have been altered, or a gain loss may have been generated or created, the transaction may not be a bond swap. Swaps are specialized transactions, often made as a result of complex mathematical calculations. The sale of bonds and the purchase of others or the use of some monies from bond sales to purchase other fixed-income securities does not necessarily qualify as a swap situation and affluent investors can engage in this activity more often than others. All investors should seek the advice of their own tax accountants and advisors.

PART 5

Managing the Affluent Investor's Financial Portfolio

CHAPTER 16

The Financial Portfolio
of the Affluent Investor

While small or average investors are usually using their earned income to live on, the affluent investor is accruing, through earned or unearned income or both, a financial portfolio of size. In other words, either through net income from savings or a combination of already purchased stocks, bonds, or other investments that throw off income in the form of interest, dividends, and capital appreciation when the investment vehicles are sold, the affluent develop financial portfolios. This income needs to be invested and also managed.

THE AFFLUENT INVESTOR AND PORTFOLIO SIZE

As noted earlier, to customize an affluent investor's portfolio and develop an investment strategy so as to take advantage of purchasing stocks and bonds in amounts that will allow for the management of that portfolio, many analysts recommend that the portfolio will be of at least $50,000 to $100,000 in size, depending on how the assets are apportioned. This is not a hard and fast rule, and in fact it depends on the size of the principal amounts of bonds that are purchased that may range from $1000 to $5000 per unit, or the cost of a share of stock that could range from less than one dollar to a few hundred dollars. Obviously, the higher the denomination that must be purchased, the fewer the number of stocks and bonds that can be bought, and therefore the less of each investment vehicle in the portfolio and the more difficult it is, when the number of securities totals only a few, to apply portfolio management techniques.

Additionally, if one were to select a portfolio of bonds because of a total aversion to stocks or whatever the reason, the total amount of funds invested that is needed to manage a bond portfolio actively as opposed to manage actively a portfolio consisting of both stocks and bonds is likely to be somewhat larger. This is so because, as noted, the cost per unit of bonds is generally higher than is the cost per unit of stock. For instance, some analysts say that an investor needs at least $15,000 to $20,000 in stocks to have a portfolio that is capable of being actively managed, but this amount may allow the purchase of only a few different bonds.

The application of all these concepts is critical for individual investors, especially for the affluent, largely because of the size of their portfolios; a small increase in the percentage of incremental total return will yield to the affluent investor a relatively large dollar amount of increased income in any given year. For instance, a 2 percent increase in the total return on an individual's portfolio of, say, $10,000 will only provide an annual increase in return of $200, but on a portfolio of $500,000, it will provide $10,000 in a given year. Furthermore, an increase of 2 percent in total return for a portfolio of $2 million will provide an annual increase in income of $40,000, and over ten years, it will be $400,000—a very substantial amount of increased income before taxes. This also does not include the amount that could be earned by investing the income as it accrues. However, the same proportionate size of a potential loss may not affect the life-style of an affluent investor as much as it would a small or average investor. If an affluent investor lost 2 percent a year in investment income, it may not be as noticeable to this individual as it would be to a smaller investor who lost the same 2 percent in income. If the loss affected the small investor's principal because the investor was forced to sell securities at less than their purchase price to pay for certain necessities, this could ultimately impact the investor's life-style.

THE INVESTMENT PROCESS FOR THE AFFLUENT

The concept described here is that the investment process for the affluent is a complex and ongoing one because of its portfolio management nature, and this sets it apart from investing by the smaller investors. Although punctuated by quarterly reviews of economic conditions, their effect on the stock and bond markets, and their impact on the investor's portfolio, the process is a continuous one, within the framework of an overall investment strategy, structured by the most appropriate risk posture of the investor, and modified over the business cycle and an individual's life cycle.

As such, the process described here encompasses the movements of money into and out of certain investments, decisions about what should be done in particular markets, when it should be accomplished, the relative speed with which it should be operationalized, and the enumerable combinations of which securities to purchase and why. Investing by the affluent is a process more than anything else, a fluid one with its thrust being thought, its milieu being the markets, and its vehicles being financial instruments. Thus, the thought process involved in investing by the affluent sets their investment activities apart from most other individual investors in both style and substance.

The investment process has distinct elements to it that form the basis of an overall investment strategy. Investment strategies, however, are not meant to be changed drastically over the economic cycle, but the asset allocations, resultant investment purchases, and perhaps even the investor's risk posture can be adjusted or readjusted. The major parts to the investment process are discussed in the sections that follow.

INITIAL OVERALL ASSET ALLOCATION

This is the first and perhaps the most critical stage in the investment process for affluent investors because they usually come to the investment table with at least a portfolio of securities that is structured in some way. Unlike the smaller investor, the affluent are not building up a portfolio or waiting for it to accrue; affluent investors usually start with a relatively good-sized asset base that is invested in a few investment vehicles. This is so especially if they have not started as yet employing a total portfolio management approach to investing. Thus, this situation presents a number of initial problems and usually entails the reallocation of the portfolio's funds to a greater or lesser degree.

First and foremost, a total asset allocation plan must be created slating certain percentages of funds to be allocated to the purchase of stocks, bonds, short-term investments, and cash vehicles. It is critical for the affluent investor, at the initial state of the portfolio improvement process, to define the appropriate cash position for the portfolio as it relates to the investors's financial needs and the present economic environment. The remainder is left for the stock, bond, and short-term portions of the portfolio that is apportioned after the economy's condition is assessed expectations about what is likely to occur in the financial markets are made, and the investor's life cycle and the risk posture are taken into account.

Then, the actual reallocation of the existing asset base into the specific sectors, in appropriate percentages, and then into precise stocks and bonds, and other investments takes place. This should occur over a period of time, perhaps over a quarter or two. It demands a review of the tax situation in the purchase and sale of each investment, together with projections for each so that, for instance, investments are not sold that are likely to produce reasonable gains in the near future.

Reallocation priorities are set by asking questions about which investment to sell first and which to purchase. This usually includes a balancing act of potential upside from a new purchase versus the potential return from holding the present one. The investor should distribute the existing asset base in a way so as not to tilt the portfolio toward investments that put the investor in an unwanted risk position or do not allow the investor to achieve the highest return commensurate with the accepted risk. At this stage, the affluent investor must also determine the stage at which the economic cycle is.

THE REALLOCATION OF ASSETS AND THE REDEPLOYMENT OF MONIES

This process is also important to the affluent investor and is much different than it is for the smaller investors. The proportion of funds are reallocated as a result of changes in the economic cycle, market expectations, and life cycle of the investor. On the economic cycle side, reallocations are made on a quarterly basis, and that means trends are evidenced and decisions are made about the reallocation of assets; redeployment takes place afterward. Economic cycles are not wedded to quarters, so the decision-making process has points within it where reallocation priorities may have to be set during quarters. Also, each stage of a cycle has a beginning and an end and, today, is often fraught with volatility. This usually of the sort that dissuades the small or average investor from staying with his or her allocations. Some affluent investors may be in the same position, but do not have to be, so reallocation and redeployment can be a longer process and occur later in each stage of the cycle.

THE ALLOCATION OF INTEREST, DIVIDENDS, AND EARNED NET INCOME

This part of the process is much different for the affluent than it is for the small or average investor, largely because of the substantial amount of funds involved and expenditures that are often made by the affluent. The smaller investor may be in some financial need, either perceived or real, so that net income is placed in a type of savings account, and the remaining income is invested in existing investments or perhaps new ones at some future date. Or most of the interest income, dividends earned, and capital gains accrued are automatically reinvested through some type of reinvestment arrangement.

For the affluent, however, these alternatives are not employed to any great extent, although they may use similar techniques. This is where the investment process of the affluent is a more fluid one. In these situations, the affluent investor must anticipate market activity so that the allocation of earned and unearned income is reinvested in varying amounts in either securities that are already owned or similar ones. Or, if change is apparent, this new capital infusion is invested in other investment vehicles that will either maximize profit-making opportunities on the upside or limit losses on the downside.

THE REDEPLOYMENT OF MONIES FROM THE LIQUIDATION OF EXISTING INVESTMENTS

This is another crucial aspect of the investment process for the affluent investor, and it comes as a result of any of five major reasons. These include changes in the investor's life cycle, problems in present investments, new investment opportunities, changes in the economic cycle, and changes in market conditions.

Conceptually, these situations are not difficult to understand and discern, but the implementation of the resultant changes in a portfolio by affluent investors usually is. The problem comes in making these changes and fitting the new securities purchases into the portfolio's asset allocation framework and doing so without changing measurably the risk posture for this individual investor at any given point in time. As a result, this effort is more pronounced and complicated for the affluent than it is for the smaller investor. Problematic investments should always be reviewed first in this redeployment process, and then recommended investment opportunities could be used to replace them. The changes in the business cycle and market conditions are more discernible and may cause redeployment more often than may changes in an investor's life cycle, especially for the affluent because their risk posture can remain constant for a longer number of years.

This part of the investment process is also difficult because the sales of investments by the affluent investor can be of large size, thus changing the total complexion of the portfolio. The portfolio's composition, therefore, must be monitored so that it is kept in line with the investor's risk posture and expectations about the stock and bond market.

INCREMENTAL BUYING AND SELLING ACTIVITY

One of the more unusual, but characteristically significant, capabilities in the investment arsenal of the affluent is the technique of purchasing and selling relatively small amounts of a given security over time as a way to "test the waters" of the accuracy of the investor's decision-making process. Not surprisingly, affluent investors can do this better than others because of the larger amount of funds they have invested at any point in time and usually because of the larger proportionate amounts they may have invested in any given security. The affluent investor may reduce the holdings of one security and use the funds to purchase another in small amounts and then await the results or returns of both holdings.

This concept is related to the allocation and redeployment procedures and processes because funds must be generated by selling securities to make new purchases. The problem in this process is overweighting a particular asset category of the portfolio with new purchases in such a way that the portfolio's overall risk posture gets out of kilter with what it was originally.

HOLDING PERIODS DURING THE ENTIRE ECONOMIC CYCLE

It should be kept in mind that throughout an economic cycle there may be certain securities that one holds regardless of the changes of the stages of the cycle and their effect on the financial markets and on the prices of the securities. This is so because of the ultimate return on these securities may be greater, over a long period of time, than on other securities, even if the market is moving against these securities for a time. Equally as important is the possibility that people of substantial means can place a greater proportion of their funds in investments that they hold for longer than average periods of time.

CHAPTER 17

The Management of Different-Sized Affluent Investor Portfolios

A concept not dealt with so far in this book is that the asset allocation for an affluent investor's financial portfolio can vary greatly, often depending on the size of the portfolio even when economic and stock and bond market conditions are not expected to change. In other words, for the same market circumstances and expectations, the asset allocation of an affluent investor's financial portfolio may be quite different, depending on the size of the portfolio. This assumes that while there is in fact a general group of investors who might be called affluent, even within this group, there are major differences in the degree of affluence that could have an impact on the way financial assets are allocated in any of these investors' portfolio, on what can be done to restructure the portfolio or a portion of it, and how this restructuring would affect the entire portfolio.

For instance, some advisors may recommend that their investors place 60 percent of their money in bonds, 30 percent of their money in stocks, and 10 percent of their money in cash. Surely, these percentages should not apply to every investor at any given point in time, whether they be affluent or not. In addition, how assets are allocated in a portfolio also depends on the size of the investor's portfolio itself, and it is the affluent investor who has the financial wherewithal to have the size of the portfolio make some difference about the way in which financial assets are allocated within it. For instance, a certain percentage of stocks in a $100,000 portfolio may mean something quite different from the same percentage of stocks in a portfolio that totals $1 million. Furthermore, whether or not the percentage of a single asset increases, or decreases, as the portfolio gets larger could markedly change the investment strategy underlying the portfolio in general and that particular asset class as a portion of the portfolio in particular.

The concepts presented here, therefore, could be applied to the equity portion of the portfolio or the fixed-income portion of the portfolio or part of either. Then each may be fine-tuned to take into account existing economic and market circumstances, the point at which individuals are in their life cycle, and their risk posture. These concepts could also be altered as the individuals' risk posture changes, as they move through their life cycle, or as their stock or bond market expectations change over time.

PORTFOLIOS OF DIFFERENT SIZES MAY DIFFER

The portfolio matrix in Table 17-1 shows five different-sized portfolios with three different scenarios as to the percentage of a particular financial asset in that portfolio as the portfolio changes in size. For the sake of discussion, it is assumed that the financial assets in the portfolio at the stated percentages are fixed-income securities and the percentages change as the portfolio increases in size. The three investors are labeled A, B, and C, respectively,

Table 17-1. Percentage of Fixed-Income
Securities of Different-Sized Portfolios
of Different Investors

Investor	Total Portfolio Assets (in $1000s)				
	$100	*$250*	*$500*	*$1000*	*$5000*
A					
Percent	20%	20%	20%	20%	20%
Amount	$ 20	$ 50	$100	$ 200	$1000
B					
Percent	20%	30%	35%	40%	45%
Amount	$ 20	$ 75	$175	$ 400	$2250
C					
Percent	45%	40%	30%	20%	10%
Amount	$ 45	$100	$150	$ 200	$ 500

denoting the three portfolios that grow in size from $100,000 to $5
million and the percentage of bonds in each portfolio at a given size.

It is also assumed that a portion of the portfolio invested in
cashlike investments in each situation, regardless of the size of the
portfolio, is 5 percent, and the percentage invested in short-term
investments is 15 percent. This means that the remainder of the
portfolio is divided between stocks and bonds. The percentages
specified in each cell of the matrix represent fixed-income securities or bonds so that the amount of the remaining percentage,
adding up to 100 percent, represents the proportion of the
portfolio that is invested in stocks.

INVESTOR A: A STEADY PROPORTIONATE COURSE

Investor A invests the same substantial percentage of funds
in investments other than bonds as the portfolio grows in size.
Indeed, 80 percent of the portfolios is invested in nonbond
vehicles and 20 percent is in fixed-income securities for every
portfolio regardless of size. At this 20 percent level, it is unlikely
that restructuring the bond portion of the portfolio could greatly
affect the overall portfolio's returns as much as if the bond portion
were a much larger proportion of the total portfolio.

Investor A cannot do that much structuring of the fixed-income portions of the portfolios that are $100,000 and $250,000 in size because of the number of bonds that can be purchased with only $20,000 and $50,000, especially if the securities purchased are in $5000 denominations. In addition, because of the sizes of the overall portfolios and perhaps also because of the proportion invested in fixed-income securities, it is likely that the fixed-income portion of the portfolio would have maturities of a relatively short duration.

The same concepts may apply to the $500,000 portfolio of investor A that has $100,000 invested in fixed-income instruments. Yet this level of investment in bonds allows for a certain amount of structuring that includes different types of fixed-income instruments, variations in credit quality, and purchases of different maturities, but not necessarily in a sequential maturities because it would be difficult to break up the $100,000 into amounts that could effectively be used to purchase securities of all 30 maturities.

Much more structuring of the fixed-income portion of the portfolio can be done with the $200,000 invested in fixed-income securities that is equivalent to 20 percent of the $1 million portfolio of investor A. Investor A also has $1 million invested in fixed-income securities of the $5 million portfolio. At this level of fixed-income investments, there is tremendous opportunity to engage in an active and effective bond portfolio management program. This can include a restructuring of the entire fixed-income portion of the portfolio, including diversification along maturity and credit-quality lines. This is not to say that these techniques cannot be employed for investor A's $100,000 and $200,000 invested in bonds in the other portfolios. Surely, some of these techniques can be employed effectively in these instances. However, the $1 million invested in fixed-income securities of the $5 million portfolio presents much more opportunities because of its size.

INVESTOR B: HIGH ON BONDS

As the size of investor B's portfolio grows from $100,000 to $5 million, the holdings of fixed-income securities increase from

20 percent to 45 percent, and the relative affect this restructuring could have on the portfolio's total return also increases. Investor B may be somewhat more risk averse than investor A, all things being equal, because of the relatively larger percentage of funds that are invested in fixed-income securities as the portfolio increases in size.

For instance, investor B has $2.25 million invested in fixed-income securities out of a $5 million total portfolio, while investor A has $1 million invested in bonds. Investor B also has $400,000 invested in bonds out of a total $1 million portfolio and $175,000 out of a total overall portfolio of $500,000. In the last two cases, there is also good opportunity for managing and restructuring the fixed-income portions of the portfolio, much more so than in similar-sized portfolios of investor A.

Investor B that has approximately $75,000 invested in bonds out of a total portfolio of $250,000. This also presents almost as many opportunities to restructure the fixed-income portion of the portfolio as does the $100,000 that investor A has invested in fixed-income securities out of a total $500,000 portfolio. The $20,000 in bonds investor B has in the $100,000 portfolio, however, leaves less room for significant bond portfolio management techniques.

INVESTOR C: PARTIAL TOWARD STOCKS

As investor C's portfolio increases from $100,000 to $5 million, the percentage of funds invested in fixed-income securities decreases from 45 percent to 10 percent. Investor C's smaller portfolios have a relatively larger percentage of funds invested in fixed-income securities, while the larger ones have a smaller percentage of funds invested in bonds. In other words, as investor C's portfolio becomes larger, the proportion of monies invested in bonds becomes smaller and the percentage of the portfolio invested in stocks becomes much larger. The larger portfolios, namely, $1 million and $5 million, have only 20 percent and 10 percent, respectively, invested in bonds.

A full 45 percent of investor C's $100,000 portfolio and 40 percent of the $250,000 one are invested bonds, or $45,000 and

$100,000, respectively. There is only a limited opportunity for restructuring the $45,000 of fixed-income securities of the $100,000 total portfolio, and a somewhat greater opportunity for restructuring the $100,000 in bonds of the $250,000 portfolio.

There are also good opportunities to restructure the fixed-income portions of the three other larger portfolios, but for the portfolio of all securities taken as a whole, the bond restructuring opportunities while significant for the largest two may not impact the portfolios substantially. This is so because of the relatively smaller amount of funds invested in fixed-income securities as a proportion of the total overall portfolio. Conversely, the effect of restructuring the $100,000 of bonds in investor C's $250,000 portfolio will likely affect this portfolio's overall return to a greater extent than will restructuring the $100,000 of bonds in investor A's $500,000 portfolio. Similar comparisons could be made of the $400,000 of bonds in investor B's $1 million portfolio and the $500,000 of bonds in investor C's $5 million portfolio.

As a result, another major point that can be deduced from this portfolio matrix is that restructuring the same dollar amount of funds invested in a particular asset class or group of securities of different-sized portfolios may or may not have the same overall effect on the entire portfolio. Rather, the ultimate effect depends on the size of each portfolio, and the relative size of asset group even if the portfolios are initially structured and then later restructured similarly.

THE CASH PORTION OF DIFFERENT-SIZED PORTFOLIOS

Related to the issues involving asset allocation of different-sized portfolios of affluent investors is the question of what percentage of cash should comprise portfolios of various sizes. As a basis for answering this question, it should be recalled that a difference of 5 percent in the asset allocation of any asset class in an overall portfolio can result in markedly different total returns of the portfolios.

For instance, if investors invest 50 percent of their financial assets in bonds and 50 percent in stocks, it is obvious that there is no money available for investments in the cash portion of the portfolio. If investors take 5 percentage points of the funds that are invested in the bond portion of the portfolios and invest those monies in cash instruments so that the asset allocation of the portfolios is 50 percent in stocks, 45 percent in bonds, and 5 percent in cash, there will be a marked difference in total return between this portfolio and the one whose funds are invested in only stocks and bonds on a 50–50 basis.

Similarly, if investors take 5 percentage points of the money that is invested in the 50 percent stock portion of the portfolio, and invest those monies in cash instruments so that the asset allocation of the portfolio is 45 percent invested in stocks, 45 percent invested in bonds, and 10 percent invested in cash, it is likely that the total return of this portfolio will greatly differ from the other two discussed here.

All things being equal, the portfolio with the largest amount of funds invested in cash financial instruments or short-term investments will be the one with the lowest overall total return over the long haul. This is a critical concept to understand, especially for the affluent investor, and it is also especially important when applied to different-sized portfolios of affluent investors.

For instance, if an affluent investor's portfolio totals $1 million and 10 percent of that portfolio is invested in cash, this means that $100,000 of the portfolio is invested in financial instruments that are highly liquid and whose funds are available for use almost immediately. However, it may not be necessary for that individual to have $100,000 in cash available all the time.

Even if an affluent investor's total portfolio totals $500,000 and 10 percent of this amount is invested in cash instruments, $50,000 will be available as liquid funds. Yet this amount of money may not be necessary to have on hand, especially when it is likely to depress the overall total return of the portfolio. However, there are investors whose portfolios are approximately $100,000 in size, and in these instances, it may be necessary for the investor to have 10 percent of it or $10,000 readily available to pay for ongoing expenses and emergencies, if they arise, regardless of whether or not this may have a depressing effect that this may have on the portfolio's total return.

This is not to say that an individual whose portfolio is $100,000 and has an income commensurate with that level of financial assets would not need less than $10,000 available at any given time. Nor does the above example imply that an individual whose portfolio hovers at approximately a $1 million would not need $100,000 or 10 percent of the portfolio available to pay for the kinds of expenses to which the individual has grown accustomed.

The point, however, is that an individual with a portfolio of $100,000 is more likely to require that approximately 10 percent of the portfolio be invested in cash instruments than it is for an individual whose portfolio is a $1 million and who also has unearned income generated by the portfolio of perhaps $50,000 to $100,000 annually as well as additional earned income that is not being spent. It is more likely, therefore, that the affluent investor with the $1 million portfolio does not need and will not want 10 percent of the portfolio, or $100,000, in available cash on hand, especially when it may greatly reduce the total return of that individual's portfolio.

Thus the percentage of an affluent investor's total financial assets that should be placed in cash instruments actually depends to a large extent on the size of the investor's total portfolio. Consequently, the concept of cash as a proportion of the total amount of invested funds or as a percentage of assets allocated is, in effect, a relative one for affluent investors. The larger that the individual investor's total portfolio is, the smaller the percentage of the portfolio that may have to, or should be, invested in cash instruments, all other things being equal, and the less likely it is that the cash portion of the portfolio will reduce the portfolio's total return. Conversely, the smaller that the portfolio of the affluent investor is, the more likely it is that the investor will need a larger relative proportion of the portfolio invested in cash at any given point in time, all other things being equal. Consequently, the more likely it is that that portfolio will register a somewhat lower total rate of return in certain markets than a larger portfolio, if both are invested in the same kinds of financial instruments and in the same proportionate amounts. This is one important reason that the affluent investor differs from, and perhaps has an advantage over, the small or average investor because of the smaller proportion of funds that the affluent investor may want to place into cash investments at any given point in time. Even within the broad spectrum of all affluent investors, the same proposition holds true if the investors' circumstances are similar.

CHAPTER 18

How to Manage an Already Structured Portion of a Portfolio

Very often, an account manager is presented with only a portion of an individual's total financial portfolio, for one reason or another, and is asked to provide investment advice that would ultimately restructure this particular part of the portfolio. In other words, an individual investor may not always bring an entire portfolio of stocks, bonds, and other investments for review, but rather only bring the stock or bond sector of it, or even simply a portion of one of these sectors. It is the affluent investor who has financial assets of sufficient size to be the most likely investor to take this option.

For instance, the individual investor requests that the municipal bond portion of the fixed-income sector of the portfolio be reviewed, or may want to reallocate and redeploy funds invested in certain types of municipal bonds, or may eventually want to restructure the entire municipal bond portion of the portfolio. This statement alone implies that there may be some type of time horizon for restructuring even a portion of a portfolio; it is not a one-step process as it might be when an investor is initially presented with an asset allocation model of how he or she might invest funds that are slated for the purchase of municipal securities. Indeed, it is rarely ever the case that investors come to the investment strategy and portfolio management table with all their assets either in relatively liquid financial instruments ready to be invested into the wide variety of investment vehicles available.

In any event, an individual's investments in a particular sector of a portfolio such as fixed-income securities, or part of a sector such as municipal bonds, may be restructured so as to provide a balance in risk, quality, or other characteristics when placed against other investments in bonds or in stocks or against the portfolio as a whole. However, restructuring a particular part of the portfolio may end up replicating the portfolio's investments in other areas so that seeking to increase the diversity of a municipal bond portion of the portfolio, for instance, together with restructuring the purchases based on some expectation of the movement of interest rates may actually be counterproductive. This may occur because the municipal portion of the portfolio was orginally structured to counterbalance other sectors of the portfolio.

For instance, if an individual invests only in long-term municipal bonds of relatively high credit quality, this strategy could be employed to balance the corporate bond portion of the portfolio that is invested in lower-quality corporate securities of short to medium maturities. This is just one example, but there are endless possible combinations of balancing acts that can occur among sectors of a portfolio.

SOME INVESTMENT GUIDELINES

Affluent investors typically purchase municipal bonds, so the municipal securities portion of the bond sector of a portfolio will be analyzed. It is assumed that the investor seeks a diversity in all respects in the purchases of municipal securities, and the highest total return available, commensurate with the most appropriate way to limit risk in terms of price and credit quality. Given these investment guidelines, the following suggestions may be appropriate for restructuring the municipal sector of the portfolio. Tax considerations for any particular investor are not factored into these guidelines.

1. Problems credit must be isolated. If necessary, they could be sold. Then, the investor may want to purchase securities of stronger credit quality.

2. The investor may want to restructure the portfolio so that there is a better balance between higher- and lower-quality municipal bonds and also take advantage of the yield spread differentials among municipals of various credit qualities.

3. The investor may then arrange the portfolio so that the securities held are in sequential maturities in proportionate amounts so as to take advantage of the direction that interest rates are expected to move.

4. The investor may also wish to restructure the portfolio to achieve a better balance between in-state and out-of-state municipal securities. However, if the investor resides in a high-tax state, he or she may want to purchase in-state municipal securities to a greater extent because of their greater after-tax yields.

5. The investor may then also wish to diversify within the municipal bond arena and purchase securities that are both revenue and general obligation bonds as well as buy different types of revenue bonds.

6. Before making any purchases or sales, the investor should also analyze the bond portfolio from a technical standpoint. The three significant areas to examine are bonds that are noncallable, refunded, and callable. They must be evaluated from a price standpoint with a view toward the projection for interest rates. The cost basis or the purchase price of these securities must be compared against their market value, both present and future, as a result of projected interest rates. The investor can then decide whether or not it is appropriate to sell any of these securities and purchase others with different coupon rates or with other qualities, or hold the securities until they actually come due or are called. Another option is to monitor interest rate movements every quarter or so and reevaluate these holdings.

Many market-related factors can impact the price and yields of fixed-income securities, but municipals particularly may be affected to a greater or lesser degree than other bonds. For instance, an increase in interest rates would force down prices of fixed-income securities. As the amount of time to the call or maturity date of a bond decreases, the prices of premium bonds move down toward par anyway, and this may be further supported by the racheting down of price as a result of an upswing in interest rates.

MAJOR QUESTIONS ABOUT A PORTION OF A PORTFOLIO

There are basically four questions that must be answered when an individual investor is expecting to evaluate and restructure a particular portion of an overall financial portfolio such as the municipal sector. The answers to all four questions involve issues relating to the development, continuance, and change in investment strategy. The questions are:

1. What is the percentage of municipal bonds in the portfolio as a proportion of the overall fixed-income portion of the portfolio?

2. Does the municipal portion of the portfolio reflect the individual investor's strategy and risk profile of the overall fixed-income portion of the portfolio?

3. What proportion of the portfolio is invested in municipals and other fixed-income securities together?

4. Do the municipal and other fixed-income portions of the portfolio, together, reflect the individual investor's investment strategy and risk posture of the entire portfolio?

Question 1

If municipals securities comprise a large proportion of the total fixed-income portion of the portfolio, the development of a strategy for investing in municipal bonds may be critical to the portfolio's total return. If municipal bonds are a small proportion of the fixed-income portfolio, a new investment restructuring strategy may not be as critical or have as great an effect on the portfolio's total return. It should be noted that investments in municipals can compensate in credit and maturity for other fixed-income securities better if the majority of investments are in governments or corporates, especially if the decision is to stick with the present allocation for any reason such as yield spread differentials among these sectors and the total return to the investor on these securities after taxes.

Key considerations in restructuring the municipal portion of the portfolio relative to the whole fixed-income portion include interest rate expectations and their likely effect on the relationship of the tax-exempt and taxable yield curves and resultant yield spreads. This includes such questions as what percentage tax-exempt securities are yielding to governments and corporates for the same maturities and, particularly in the case of corporate securities, for the same credit qualities. All these considerations also must be evaluated if the taxable section of the portfolio is being isolated and restructured as the dependent variable in relation to the independent variable, namely, the tax-exempt portion of the fixed-income portfolio.

Question 2

Another issue is the extent to which the municipal portion of the portfolio does or does not reflect the investor's strategy and risk posture for the fixed-income portion of the entire portfolio. The characteristics of the municipal portion could mirror those of the fixed-income portion of the portfolio, or it could complement it. However, restructuring the municipal portion of the portfolio to change the distribution of the maturity spectrum without taking into account the rest of the fixed-income portion of the portfolio could alter the investor's strategy for the fixed-income section of the portfolio.

For instance, if the municipal portfolio was basically structured with long maturities, corporate securities could have made up the intermediate maturities because of yield spread relationships at the time of purchase. The shorter maturities could have been comprised of government securities because of yield spread relationships or simply impending or episodic needs for capital by the individual investor. In this instance, the amount of securities in various maturities could, when the fixed-income portion of the entire portfolio is taken together, be fairly evenly proportioned, showing that the investor expected interest rates to stabilize over the near term. As a result, changes in the maturity structure of the municipal section could alter the strategic positioning of the whole fixed-income portion of the portfolio. Restructuring the municipal portion could also change the investor's risk posture, income streams, and the amount of tax-exempt interest income received.

Question 3

It is also critical to discern the amount of funds invested in the municipals together with fixed-income portions of the portfolio as a proportion of the amount invested in the entire portfolio. If the fixed-income portion of the portfolio, including municipal securities, is a large proportion of the total portfolio, restructuring the municipal portion as well as the fixed-income portfolio as a whole may be important and constructive. This should be done for diversity by working with credit, maturity, and income stream factors to take advantage of market forces affecting yield spreads. With a large amount of funds invested in fixed-income securities by affluent investors, restructuring the fixed-income portion of the portfolio may be a critical task.

This restructuring, however, should also be done with a view toward the investment strategy underlying the purchases of stocks, short-term investments, and cash. The extent to which it should take the stock strategy into account or will affect the overall portfolio depends on the relative proportion of funds invested in each group of securities. For instance, if the stock portion of the portfolio is large in size in relation to the rest of the portfolio, especially the fixed-income portion, restructuring the fixed-income portion of the portfolio, or even the municipal one, with certain parameters, will probably not have as great an affect on the portfolio's overall rate of return. If there is roughly an even division between the amount of funds of an individual investor's portfolio invested in both fixed-income securities and stocks, restructuring the fixed-income portion could still prove advantageous. The extent to which restructuring the municipal portion will impact the total portfolio depends on the size of it in proportionate relation to the overall portfolio, its various sectors, and each one's strategic positioning.

Question 4

Another major question that must be answered is the extent to which the municipal and the rest of the fixed-income portion of the overall portfolio is or is not reflective of the individual investor's investment strategy and risk profile as a whole. For small investors, this question may not be quite as critical as it is for affluent ones. If it is reflective, any diversification or restructuring efforts would have to generally be somewhat less drastic to coincide with the investment strategy underlying the rest of the portfolio. If it is not reflective of the portfolio, as a whole, there may also be reasons why this is so, but there may be greater opportunities to alter the fixed-income portion of the portfolio in risk posture and overall investment strategy.

This can be done through changes in a single sector, like the municipal one, if it is a large enough proportion of the overall portfolio. Put differently, the alteration or restructuring of the fixed-income portion of the portfolio, including the municipal sector, must take into account the overall investment strategy. Then decisions must be made regarding the extent to which the original balance should be kept, based on interest rate expectations and with an underlying view as to what may or may not occur in the stock market thus affecting the whole portfolio.

LOOKING AT THE TOTAL PORTFOLIO

The point of this discussion is that in restructuring any portion of an individual investor's portfolio, especially an affluent investor's whose investments in sheer dollar amounts may be markedly large, the investor must take into account the investment strategy of the overall portfolio, the risk profile and market expectations that are demonstrated by the portfolio's investments, and the part that the particular portion of the portfolio to be restructured plays in the investment strategy underlying the entire portfolio. Also, the effect that changes in that particular portion of the portfolio would have on the portfolio as a whole is a critical dimension of this evaluation.

How any portion of a portfolio is restructured also depends on the amount of cash or short-term investments the investor has on hand. In addition, as a restructuring of a portion of the portfolio occurs, greater or lesser amounts of cash or short-term investments could accrue as a necessary or desired result. This could change the overall investment strategy and total rate of return rather quickly, and this is something to monitor closely. No portion of a portfolio can be altered without affecting the portfolio as a whole so that an understanding of the investor's entire portfolio is critical to restructuring a portion of it.

CHAPTER 19

Conclusion: Investment Strategy Blueprints for the Affluent Investor

A single volume obviously cannot cover every investment strategy for every situation in the financial markets for every investor, or even for a single investor group. Each situation and investor is different, and each requires special attention beyond what any book or computer program can possibly provide.

However, by isolating a particular kind of individual investor, such as the affluent one, from the general group of individual investors, and then delving into the construction of his or her financial portfolio at different points in the investor's life and for affluent investors with different risk postures, it becomes increasingly apparent that certain investment strategies for asset allocation and the purchases and sales of individual securities emerge. These recommendations are surely not the end-all and be-all of investment strategies for all affluent investors. No financial writer or investment manager could possibly perform such a task, especially when an individual's taxes are a very important consideration in the overall investment process and are beyond the scope of this volume.

To a greater or lesser degree, the investment scenarios and hypothetical portfolio constructs presented here may be viewed as a basic skeletal framework on which specific tailor-made strategies are ultimately created for each investor of substantial assets and/or income. Unless this conceptual framework that includes taking into account expected economic scenarios and stock and bond market movements is understood in the way they affect one another, it is very difficult at best, and nearly impossible at worst, to fine-tune these investment strategies for specific affluent investors. As basic frameworks of concepts, these proposed hypothetical investment strategies provide readers and investors alike with a way of thinking about the investment process. Ultimately, however, myriad permutations and combinations of investment strategies and the selection of particular financial instruments for purchase can be made.

THE AFFLUENT INVESTOR'S PERSPECTIVE: THROUGH THE EYES OF THE CUSTOMER

As a sociological group, the affluent exist to some extent in a world of their own. Their world and their view of the world around them, of necessity, collides with their financial requirements and their investment needs, desires, and expectations. It must, therefore, be true that even from the most basic economic and market phenomena to the most complicated and volatile ones, their beliefs as to what could be done to take advantage of these situations from a risk-reward perspective could be markedly different than those investors of lesser means.

This is not to say that, from an investment perspective, all affluent investors are identical in all ways all of the time, or that they, as a group, are generally homogeneous. Nothing could be farther from the truth. Nevertheless, similar investment products may look different to them than they do when seen through the eyes of the small or average investor, and, when purchased in varying quantities, these securities could mean much more or much less to the affluent from a risk perspective. Also, on an overall investment strategy level, asset allocation and the resultant purchases of different types of securities in varying quantities may either mean something different to affluent investors or affect them emotionally and their investment strategy concretely in ways that may not be comparable to those of the smaller or average investor.

The clear conclusion is that all these strategies and investment vehicles are not different simply because of their standing in the marketplace, but rather that they may mean drastically different things to investors who purchase or sell them. Indeed, important dichotomies in the overall group of individual investors are the difference between the affluent group, on the one hand, and the smaller investor, on the other; what investment strategies and financial vehicles mean to each; and how they affect each group's overall total return of their portfolios.

Stated somewhat differently, investment products, asset allocation models, and investment strategies should be different for the affluent investor because they are seen, reviewed, analyzed, and evaluated through the eyes of a much different kind of person. Each affluent investor is also different. Even when the income and assets of a group of affluent investors are roughly the same, no computer-driven model could spew forth the appropriate investment strategies and asset allocation models that each individual investor in that group should pursue. Each affluent investor is different, and what may be appropriate for one may be inappropriate for another.

At best, a computer model that provides a possible way to allocate an affluent investor's financial assets and at a given point in time in the economic or business cycle must also take into account the individual's preferences for all these investments and expectations about what is to come in the financial markets, both stock and bond. Computerizing an individual's financial situation is a help and is often used as a first step, but there are many more steps to follow before an investment strategy is decided on and the financial securities are selected for purchase and sale.

This is especially important because most investment reviews are conducted on an already structured portfolio; few individual investors come to the table with all their funds in cash accounts that can be dispersed immediately into the appropriate asset groups and then be used to purchase the recommended securities in the recommended amounts. Such a situation is a pure case and usually occurs only when an individual sells a business, inherits an asset and sells it, or inherits a large amount of funds that are invested in relatively liquid financial instruments.

WHY THE PRODUCT MUST FIT THE CUSTOMER

As a result of the foregoing considerations, the investment process is thus stood on its head and rightly so. It is not whether the stock or bond is a good one at a given point in time or whether the stock market is going up so that certain stocks may be appropriate investments, or even if interest rates are expected to move downward so that the bond portion of the portfolio should be lengthened and funds should be invested in bonds of longer maturities. The first step is, in fact, the analysis of the investment climate and the expected one, but it must then be evaluated from the point of view of an individual investor, as one of a group. Only then can a product be placed within that framework of appropriate investment strategies, and thus investments can then be made from the customer's standpoint.

Products, therefore, become the dependent variable rather than the independent one. The fit between product and customer is not based first on research recommendations or some type of right investment, but rather on what is right for a particular investor group as seen from a specific customer's perspective. This is then tempered by an assessment of the overall investment climate and what investments are most likely to be the most appropriate at this given point in time.

It is also important that the overall assets of the affluent investor be taken into account when investment strategies are developed and if and when they are changed over time. Often the sale of a piece of real estate, an impending tax liability, or an unexpected increase in business income can result in the alteration of one's investment perspective. Affluent investors also have episodic needs for capital or the psychological expectation that a certain proportion of their funds be made available and be spent on items of apparent importance to them. These situations may change the investment parameters of the affluent investor enormously and quickly. They may also change the temperament of the investor for a given time period.

If this occurs, the investor must place these new parameters within the structure of their overall investment strategy and compare and contrast their new needs or expectations with those that were previously developed with great forethought over time. This may result in an overall change in investment strategy, and it may even alter, perhaps just for the time being, the risk posture of an affluent investor.

These changes may be evaluated between or during the quarterly assessments of the affluent investor's overall portfolio and investment strategy or they may be held in abeyance for the time of annual review. Nevertheless, it is much more likely that an affluent investor will be subject to either larger episodic needs for capital or the sudden increases in amount of available funds for investment than would a small or average investor. As a result, these concerns and opportunities must be placed within the confines of their previously well-thought-out investment programs—one that fits product and customer.

TOWARD AN INDIVIDUALIZED INVESTMENT STRATEGY

The major goal of the investment world and also of the academic one might be to bridge the gap created by each by making the development of an investment strategy and the selection of investment instruments processes that are understandable. Most would agree that this means, in part, turning complicated financial and economic data into a digestable form, and generally this may be so, but it is only a small portion of the entire investment process. The goal actually, and perhaps more important, involves developing a thought process as to how to create an overall investment strategy and select particular investment vehicles for purchase and sale over the course of a business cycle as seen through the eyes of a specific investor within a particular investor group. It thus turns the investment process around so that it is not appropriate to say that certain investment strategies are appropriate or that particular stocks or bonds are good investments. The question that should actually be asked is: Do they promise the greatest return for the given amount of risk within a particular stage of an economic cycle and point at which an individual investor is in his or her life cycle with particular levels of income and assets and expectations about the markets?

It is, therefore, the customer that must be focused on first and last and what the economic and financial world means to that particular investor. Then there must be developed an overall strategy for that particular investor group, for their asset allocations over given parts of the business cycle, and then, deviations from that skeletal framework must be created for each individual based on the investments that are available in the marketplace and their relative rates of return, and each investor's risk postures and financial needs and expectations.

Investors should not be asked, for instance, if they want to purchase a very good stock. Rather, investors should be asked whether they have an investment strategy at this point in their lives, and in the present economic environment, with a certain expectation of what is likely to come in the financial markets, so that a particular stock would be a good purchase as opposed to others that are available or others that are presently in their portfolio.

With this perspective, the pieces of the investment puzzle are placed on the table and are used until the complete picture is identified. In any event, perhaps more than any other individual investor, the affluent one is the one likely to gain most from the view of the investment process depicted here.

Index